GCSE

Design & Technology Resistant Materials

Complete Revision and Practice

Contents

Section One — The Design Process

Section Two — Tools and Processes

Section Three — Materials and Components

Section Four — Systems and Mechanisms

Contents

Section Five — Market Influences

Section Six — Industrial Awareness

Section Seven — Project Advice

Published by Coordination Group Publications Ltd.

Editors:
Vicky Brereton, Simon Little.

Contributors:
Martin Chester, Charley Darbishire, Stephen Guinness, Brian Kerrush, Becky May, John Nicolls, Andy Park, Katherine Reed, Julie Schofield, Emma Singleton, Karen Steel, Claire Thompson, James Wallis, Chrissy Williams.

With thanks to Richard Grier for the proofreading.

AQA material is reproduced by kind permission of the Assessment and Qualifications Alliance.

Edexcel examination questions are reproduced by kind permission of Edexcel Ltd.

OCR examination questions are reproduced by kind permission of OCR.

ISBN-10: 1 84146 381 7
ISBN-13: 978 1 84146 381 0
Website: www.cgpbooks.co.uk
Printed by Elanders Hindson Ltd, Newcastle upon Tyne.
Clipart from CorelDRAW®

Text, design, layout and original illustrations © Coordination Group Publications Ltd. 2003
All rights reserved.

Design Brief

The process of designing and making something is called 'the design process'. The whole process can take a while — so it's usually broken down into smaller chunks.

*The **design process** is similar in **industry** and **school***

It's no accident that the things you'll have to do for your Design and Technology project are similar to what happens in industry.

- The best products in industry are those that address a real need.
- That's why companies spend so much time and money on customer research. The more people there are who would actually use a product, the more chance it stands of being a roaring success.
- The best ideas for Design and Technology projects are also those that meet a genuine need.

The rest of this section describes a typical design process. It shows the sort of thing that happens in industry every day. It also shows the stages you need to go through while you're putting a Design and Technology project together.

*First get your **idea** for a **new product***

Whether you're working in the research and development department of a multinational company, or you're putting together your project, you need to explain why a new product is needed. It could be for one of the following reasons:

1) There are problems with an existing product.
2) The performance of an existing design could be improved.
3) There's a gap in the market that you want to fill.

*The **design brief** explains **why** your product is **needed***

The design brief explains why there might be a need for a new product. It should include the following:

1) an outline of the problem and who it affects
2) the need arising from the problem
3) what you intend to do about it (e.g. design and make...)
4) how your product will be used
5) the environment it will be used in

Basically, the design brief should concentrate on the problem you're trying to solve.

Your design brief should start by describing the problem

Your design brief should be simple and concise. A design brief should not be a detailed description of what you intend to make — you can only say this after you've designed it and tried things out. Describe the problem first. The rest comes later.

Research

Once you've written your design brief, you can start researching your project.

Research can help you get ideas

It's worth doing your research carefully — it can give you lots of ideas for the rest of the design process. The point of doing research is to:

1) check that people will actually want your product (although you might have done this already when you chose your project).
2) find out what makes an existing product good or bad — talk to people who actually use this kind of product, and see what they like or dislike.
3) find out the materials, pre-manufactured components and techniques that you can use, and how they will affect the manufacturing and selling costs.
4) give you a good starting point for designing.

There are different kinds of research

You can do different kinds of research. This might include:

① **Questionnaires** — to find out people's likes/dislikes and so on. This will help you identify your target group and find out market trends (e.g. what things are becoming more popular).

② **Disassembling a product** (i.e. taking it apart) — this will help you find out how a current product is made and how it works. It could also give you information about different materials and processes used, and how existing products meet potential users' needs.

③ **Measuring** — to find out the weights and sizes of current products. This might give you an idea of the possible size, shape and weight of your product. You could also do some kind of sensory analysis (e.g. you could see how it feels and looks).

Research analysis means drawing conclusions

Once you've done your research, you'll need to come to some conclusions. This means deciding how to use the information to help you with your design. This is called research analysis.

Try to do the following:

1) Pick out the useful information.
2) Explain what impact the research will have on your designs.
3) Suggest ways forward from the research gathered.

By the time you've done all this, you should have some ideas about how to tackle your project.

You can never have too many ideas

Research is important. You could spend some time doing 'book research', e.g. finding out about any British or European standards your product will have to meet. The Internet is a useful research tool at this stage.

Design Specification

Once you've picked out the main points of your research, you're ready to put together a design specification.

The *design specification* is a *list* of *conditions to meet*

1) The design specification is based on your research.
2) It is more detailed than the design brief.
3) The design specification gives a list of features and standards that your product should meet.
4) Try to put your specification together in bullet form as specific points.

> E.g. if your research tells you that people would never buy a backscratcher weighing 300 grams or more, then your design specification might include the statement, "Must weigh less than 300 grams."

5) Include some or all of the following:

- a description of how it should look
- details about what it has to do/be
- materials, ingredients and joining methods
- details of size/weight
- safety points to consider
- financial constraints

Compare your designs with the design specification

1) Once you've come up with a design, you need to compare it to the specification and confirm that each point is satisfied.

E.g. If your design specification contains these two points, then all of your designs should be at least 400 mm long and have a variety of colours.

E.g. • The minimum length will be 400 mm.
• The product should be multicoloured.

2) Some points might be harder to compare to your specification simply by looking at the product design.

E.g. • The product should feel comfortable.

For this, you'll need to get someone to test the product once it's been made/modelled.

You might need to make *more than one* specification

You'll probably need to produce several specifications as your project develops:

> Initial Design Specification — this is your first design specification. It should be done after your research analysis.

1) As you develop your design, you'll probably want to make some changes to your design specification. This is fine, as long as your design brief is being met and you have taken your research analysis into account.
2) Maybe as a result of some of your modelling (see page 5) you'll find that certain materials aren't suitable. You can add this information to an updated specification.
3) You can keep doing this until you end up with a final product specification.

The design specification is where you use your research

Making a design specification is a vital step in designing and manufacturing a new product. So learn about it.

Generating Proposals

This is where it all gets a bit more interesting. This is the creative bit, where you start generating ideas.

There are a few **tricks** that can help you **get started**

The following are suggestions to help you get started with designing:

1) Create a mood board — this is a collection of different images, words, materials, colours and so on that might trigger ideas for your design.
2) Brainstorm — think up key words, questions and initial thoughts relating to your product. (Start off by just writing whatever ideas come into your head — analyse them later.)

A simple spider diagram can really help to identify what needs to be researched.

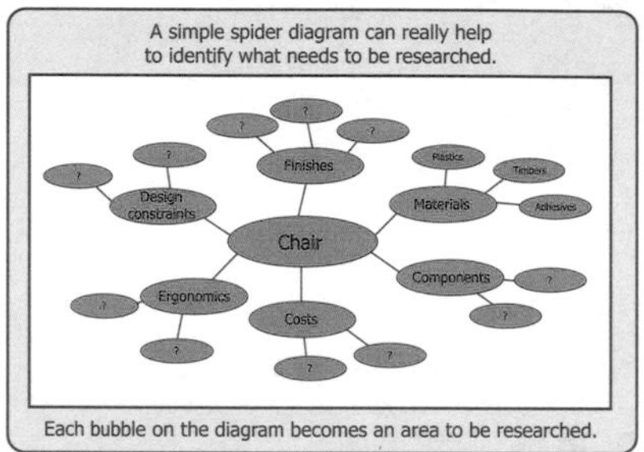

Each bubble on the diagram becomes an area to be researched.

3) Work from an existing product — but change some of its features or production methods so that it fits in with your specification.
4) Break the task up into smaller parts — e.g. design the 'look' of the product (aesthetics), then look at the technology involved and so on.

You need to come up with a **range of designs**

1) You need to annotate (i.e. add notes to) your designs to fully explain your ideas, e.g. about:

- materials
- shape
- production method
- size
- cost
- functions
- user
- advantages and disadvantages

2) You need to produce a wide range of appropriate solutions that you think could actually be made.

3) Try to use a range of techniques for presenting your designs — for example:

- perspective drawing
- orthographic projection
- cross-sections
- freehand sketching
- digital camera photos
- isometric projection
- Computer-Aided Design (CAD)

4) Once you've got a few possible designs, you need to check that each one matches your specification — any that don't will not be suitable.

5) Finally, you need to choose one of your suitable designs to develop further.

Remember — all your ideas have to match your specification

Think about what someone will need to know to fully appreciate your design, and include this information on your proposal. And remember — you need to do quite a few of these so that you can choose the best one to develop and improve. This is the time to get creative.

Development

Once you've decided on a design, you can begin to develop it further.
This is when your design should really start to take shape.

You can **develop** your design in **different ways**

Depending on the type of product that's being produced, further development might involve:

1) producing further sketches — but in more detail, e.g. recording the sizes of fittings and components, and dimensions for component positions. Also sketching how parts should be constructed and fitted together.
2) modelling your idea. This lets you test that it works and also allows you to experiment with different aspects of the design. E.g. you could try various materials, sizes and production methods.
3) using people's opinions about developments to help you arrive at a satisfactory solution.

Modelling means **trying** things out

It can be useful to prototype or model your idea, especially if it's difficult to draw.

1) Try out different aspects of your design. If your design is quite complex it may help to break it down into smaller, more manageable parts and test them individually.
2) Use a camera (digital or otherwise) to record your models.
3) Evaluate the models (see next page), identifying reasons for selecting or rejecting different designs.

This is a vital part of the design process. Ideally you should solve all the potential problems with your design at this stage.

Use the **results** to make **modifications**

1) Results from your modelling and from your evaluation (see next page) will help you make important modifications (changes) to improve the product, and help it meet the design specification.
2) Suggested improvements could be:
   - ways to make the product itself better,
   - suggestions to make it more suitable for mass production (see page 101).
3) But make sure you keep a record of whatever it is you find out (see next page).
4) Once you've made a modification to your design, you'll need to try it out to see if it actually improves things.
5) You might find that you end up modifying something, then trying it out, then making another modification and trying that out, then making another modification and trying that out, and so on.

Modelling is more useful than you'd think

Modelling and evaluation (see next page) go hand in hand. It's pointless building a model and trying it out if you're not going to learn anything from it. So keep thinking about and evaluating your work at all times.

Evaluation

Evaluation is an important part of any product development process.
It needs to be done at various stages along the way.

Keep **records** of your **research** and **testing**

1) As you develop your product, keep records of any testing or market research you do. Write it all down, keep it, and refer back to it.
2) You might have tested materials for suitability, or tested components to see how well they work — but whatever you did, you need to write down all the results.
3) Compare the good and bad points of existing products with your model or prototype. Ask yourself if your product does the job better. Record your results.
4) Find out people's opinions and preferences about your models and prototypes (see previous page). This will help you to refine your ideas so you can arrive at the best solution.
5) Questionnaires help here — relevant market research questions might include:

- Does the product work well?
- Does the product work as well as similar products on the market?
- Does the product look good? Is it well styled and modern-looking?
- Are you unsure about any of the features? If so, which ones and why?
- If this product were on the market, would you consider buying it?
- If you were buying it, which price range do you think it would fall into?
- Do you prefer another similar product to this one?

This type of evaluation is called formative evaluation — it's being used to help form the final design.

You should know **exactly** what you're making

By the time you've finished developing your ideas and have arrived at a final design, you should have found out / worked out:

1) The best materials, tools and other equipment to use (and their availability). This might include identifying any pre-manufactured components you're going to use.
2) The approximate manufacturing time needed to make each item.
3) How much it should cost to manufacture each item.
4) The most appropriate assembly process — this is going to be important information when it comes to planning production, and can be in the form of a flow chart (see page 8).

If you don't know what you're doing now, you never will

At this stage of the process it should be crystal clear in your own mind how your final product should look, and how you're going to make it. But you're not finished yet. There's still the little business of actually making your pride and joy.

Manufacturer's Specification

Now that you know exactly what you're going to make, you need to communicate all that information to the person who's actually going to make it.

You need to produce a *manufacturer's specification*

A manufacturer's specification can be a written series of statements, or working drawings and sequence diagrams. It has to explain exactly how the product will be made, and should include:

1) clear construction details explaining exactly how each bit's going to be made,
2) sizes — precise measurements of each part,
3) tolerances — the maximum and minimum sizes each part should be,
4) finishing details — any special sequences for finishing,
5) quality control instructions — where, when and how the manufacturing process and product quality should be checked.
6) costings — how much each part costs, and details of any other costs involved.

Spreadsheets are great for working out costings

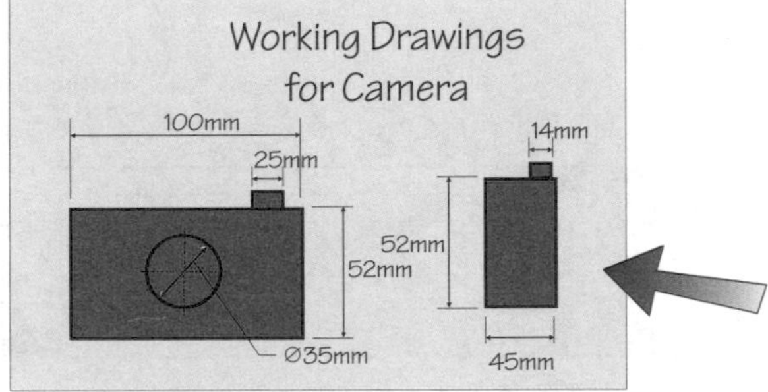

Working drawings give the precise dimensions of the product.

Plan how long the *production process* should take

When you get to this stage of product development, you also need to plan:

1) how your methods might have to change to manufacture the product in volume
2) each stage of the process in a great deal of detail
3) how long each stage will take
4) what needs to be prepared before you can start each stage
5) how you will ensure consistency and quality

See the next page as well for some different ways to help with this planning.

The devil's in the detail

This part of the design process is about detail and precision. Your manufacturer's specification has to be spot on, or you end up wasting a lot of time and wasting materials.

Planning Production and Evaluation

Making one or two examples of your product is (relatively) easy. But mass-producing it is a whole different ball game. And it takes a lot of careful planning.

Use **charts** to help you

You need to work out how long each stage will take, and how these times will fit into the total time you've allowed for production. There are different ways of doing this:

1) Work Order
   This can be produced as a table or flow chart. The purpose of a work order is to plan in sequence each task to be carried out. This will also include: tools and equipment, quality control stages, safety, and so on.

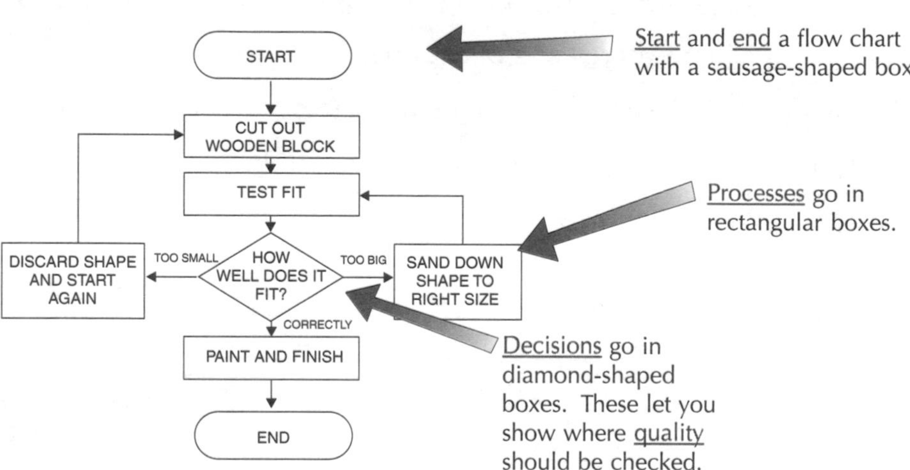

2) Gantt Chart
   This is a time plan showing the management of tasks. The tasks are listed down the left-hand side, and the timing plotted across the top. The filled in squares show how long each task takes, and the order they're done in.

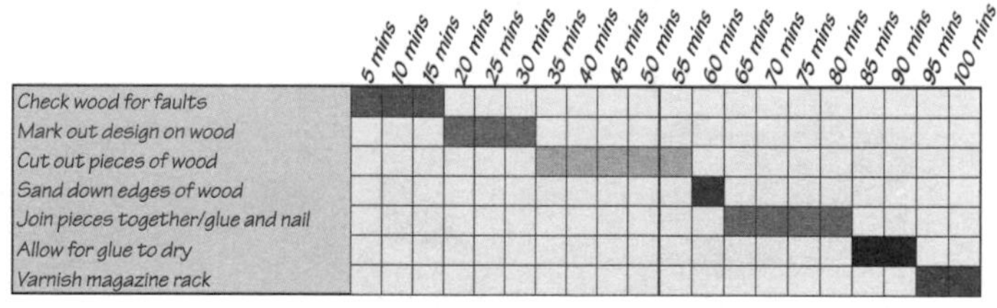

Test *that the product* ***works*** *and meets the* ***specification***

1) When you think you've got the final product, it's vital to test it. Most important of all, you have to make sure it works, and meets the original design specification.

2) More questionnaires or surveys may help here. Ask a wide range of people to give their opinions about the finished product.

3) If your product fails to match any part of the specification, you must explain why. You really have to stand back and have a good hard think about your work. If you aren't satisfied with the way any part of the process went, think of how you could put it right for next time.
   Write it down in the form of a report.

4) This type of final evaluation is called summative evaluation — it summarises what you've learnt.

Proper planning is a big time saver

So, that's all you have to do when it comes to your project.
In a few short weeks you can achieve what people in industry take several months to do.

Warm-Up and Worked Exam Questions

These warm-up questions should ease you gently in and make sure you've got the basics straight. If there's anything you've forgotten, check up on the facts before you do the exam questions.

Warm-up Questions

1) Explain what a design brief should include.
2) When researching a project, why might you disassemble an existing product?
3) Give four points that should be included in a design specification.
4) What is a mood board?
5) What is a prototype?
6) Write down three examples of questions you might include in a questionnaire to evaluate a new product.
7) What should be in a manufacturer's specification?
8) Draw a Gantt chart for making a jam sandwich.

Exam questions are the best way to practise what you've learnt — they're exactly what you'll have to do on the big day. Read carefully through this worked example, then try the questions on the next page.

Worked Exam Question

1 The diagram below shows a wooden toy train, designed for children aged 2-5 years.

<u>Main Features</u>

Yellow painted finish.

Windows and doors painted on.

Moveable wheels

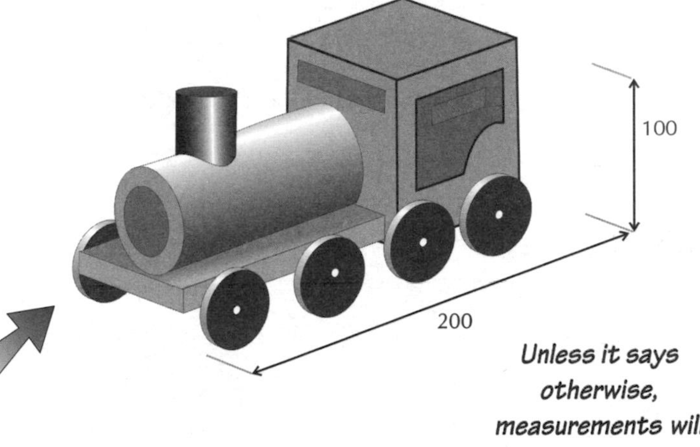

Look at the main features of the toy — why would children <u>like</u> to play with it, and why is it <u>safe</u> for them to use?

Unless it says otherwise, measurements will ALWAYS be in mm.

Give three ways in which the design is suitable for children aged 2-5 years.

1 *Moveable wheels allow the toy to be pushed or rolled along a surface, making the toy more interesting to play with.*

(1 mark)

2 *No small parts that could be pulled off and present a choking hazard, e.g. windows and doors painted on instead.*

(1 mark)

3 *Brightly painted finish makes the toy look fun and attractive.*

(1 mark)

Exam Questions

2 A cutlery storage tray is required to store forks, knives and spoons.
A manufacturer has produced the design below.

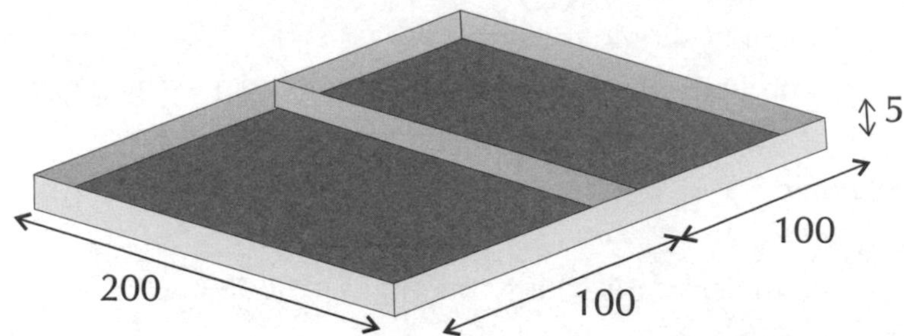

(a) Give **two** pieces of information you should find out before designing the cutlery tray.

1 ....

(1 mark)

2 ....

(1 mark)

(b) Suggest **two** ways in which the tray shown fails as a design solution.

1 ....

(1 mark)

2 ....

(1 mark)

(c) Use notes and sketches to show **two** modifications that could be made to improve the design above.

(4 marks)

(d) Suggest **two** ways you could test whether the storage tray has achieved its purpose.

1 ....

(1 mark)

2 ....

(1 mark)

Exam Questions

3 The diagram below shows a computer user sitting in a tall chair.

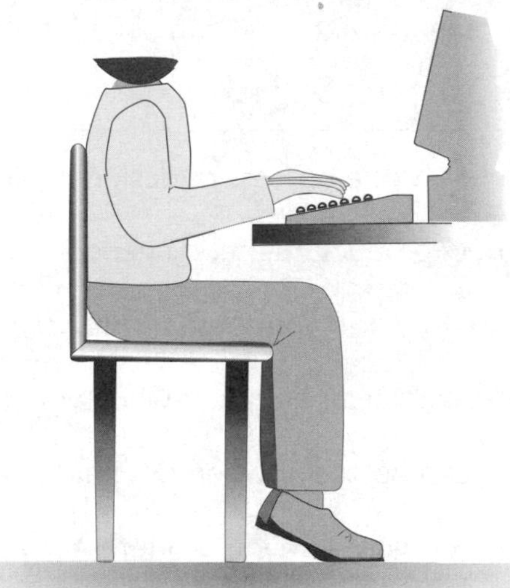

A manufacturer is investigating how comfortable a group of computer users are at their desks. One of the computer users says that he has problems resting his feet flat on the polished floor, when sitting in a tall chair.

A foot rest is required which will raise the computer user's feet and support them at an angle of 20° on the polished floor.

Complete the following design specification.
Include four more conditions for the foot rest.

The foot rest:

1 must support the users feet at an angle of 20°.

2 ....

(1 mark)

3 ....

(1 mark)

4 ....

(1 mark)

5 ....

(1 mark)

Revision Summary for Section One

Try the revision questions, and then have a look back through the section to see if you got them all right. If you did — great. But if you got any wrong, have another careful read of the section and then try the questions again. And keep doing this until you can get all the questions right. That way, you know you're learning...

1) What is the name given to the whole process of designing and making something?
2) Give three reasons why a new product might be needed.
3) Describe five things you should put in your design brief.
4) Give three ways in which research can help you when you're designing a new product.
5) Explain how questionnaires can be useful when designing or researching a product.
6) Give two other methods you could use to carry out research.
7) What is the name given to the process of drawing conclusions from your research?
8) Explain what is meant by a design specification.
9) Give six details about a product that should be included in a design specification.
10) When would you compile an initial design specification?
11) Give three ways of generating ideas.
12) What does the word 'annotate' mean?
13) What information should you include in your designs?
14) Why should you aim to produce a number of design ideas?
15) Give three different drawing techniques you could use for presenting your designs.
16) Name two ways of developing your designs further.
17) Explain why it's useful to model your designs.
18) Describe two kinds of improvement you could make to your design.
19) When should you evaluate your design? a) at the end of the project
    b) throughout the project c) at the start of the project.
20) Describe two ways of evaluating your work.
21) What is meant by the phrase 'formative evaluation'?
22) Explain why a manufacturer's specification needs to be very precise.
23) Give four kinds of information that need to be on a manufacturer's specification.
24) When using a Gantt chart, what information goes down the left-hand side?
25) Describe two methods of planning how long the manufacturing process should take.
26) What is a 'summative evaluation'?

Hand Tools

It's not all high-tech stuff in this section. You need to know about hand tools too.

Saws are the main cutting tools

1) Different saws have teeth designed for cutting different materials.
2) Tenon saws, ripsaws and cross-cut saws are used on wood. Ripsaws are used for cutting in the direction of the grain, cross-cut saws are used for cutting across the grain.
3) Hacksaws are used for cutting metals and plastics.
4) Coping saws can be used on either wood or plastic, and are mainly for cutting curves.
5) Saws have to be kept sharp, either by sharpening (e.g. tenon saw) or replacing the blade (e.g. coping saw).

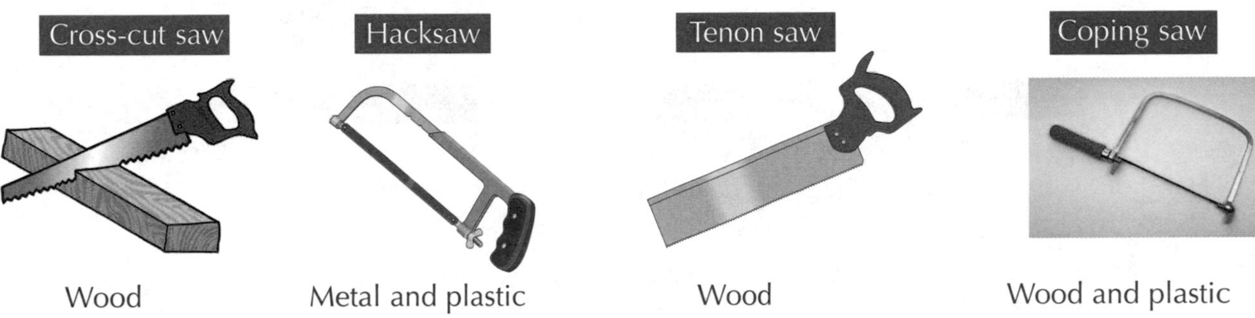

Wood — Metal and plastic — Wood — Wood and plastic

Planes and files are used for shaping and smoothing

Planes are for wood

1) This is a bench plane:

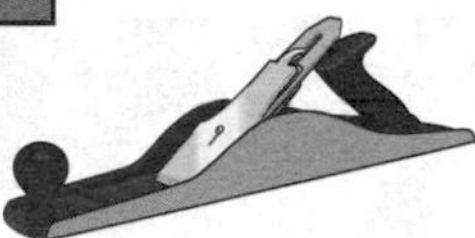

2) It has an angled blade that shaves off thin layers of material.
3) It's used on wood for removing material (shaping).

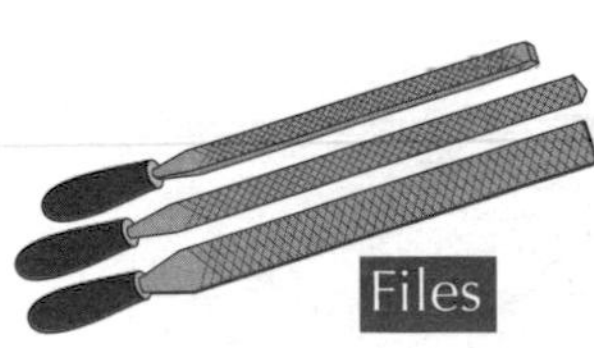

You can get files for most materials

1) Files have hundreds of small teeth to cut away at a material.
2) Different cuts of file make them suitable for different processes: rough cuts are for removal of material, fine cuts are for finishing (final smoothing).
3) Most files are meant for metals and plastics, but there are special ones with very coarse teeth called cabinet rasps for use on wood.

Make sure you learn which saw is which...

Before removing material always mark out what's to be removed and then double-check your marking out. You don't want to be sticking pieces of your project back together again.

Hand Tools

In your exam and project you'll be expected to give specific instructions — not just "drill a hole". There are lots of different drills, bits and chisels — always say which one you're using.

Drills are for making holes

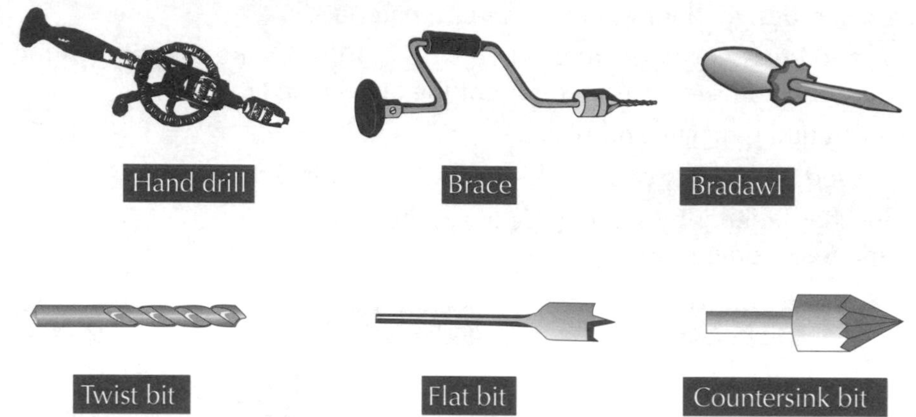

1) Hand drills, braces and bradawls are hand tools for making holes. There are also machine drills and hand-held power drills.
2) All drills rotate the drill bit clockwise and press it against the material.
3) Twist bits are used for drilling small holes into wood, metals and plastics.
4) Flat bits are used on wood and plastics to drill large flat-bottomed holes.
5) Countersink bits make holes for screw heads to sit in.
6) Different bits are suitable for different materials. Auger bits are used on wood. High speed steel (HSS) twist bits are used on metals and plastics.

Chisels are used for shaping woods and metals

1) Chisels are used to cut away and shape materials.
2) Wood chisels (bevel-edged, firmer and mortise chisels) are used on wood and are hit with a mallet.
3) Cold chisels are used on metals and are hit with a hammer.
4) Gouges are chisels with a curved cutting edge — they're used for sculpting.

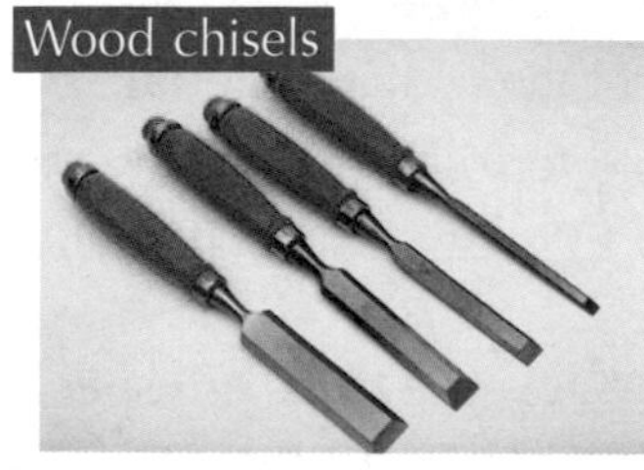
Wood chisels

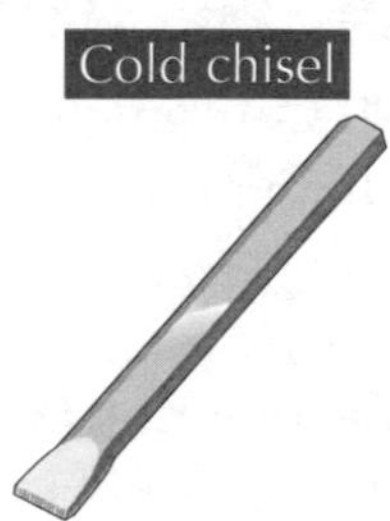
Cold chisel

Gouges

Learn the names and the uses for each of these tools

There are a few new terms to learn here — It's important to get them learnt for the exam. Knowing your tools also means that you'll be able to chose the right one for the job when you're doing your project.

Machine Tools

Machine tools do the same jobs as manual tools — but more efficiently.

Machine tools are quick and accurate

1) These are usually stationary and are often bolted to the workbench or the floor.
2) They can be used for processing large quantities of material accurately and quickly.
3) Most machines used for wood are attached to a dust extractor.
4) Safety glasses should be used and clothing tucked in to avoid it catching in machines.

There are different types of automatic saw

Whether you have these saws in your D&T workshop or not, you still need to know that they exist and what they are used for.

The circular saw or saw bench has a round blade and is used to cut wood and man-made wooden materials like plywood to size. It makes straight cuts only.

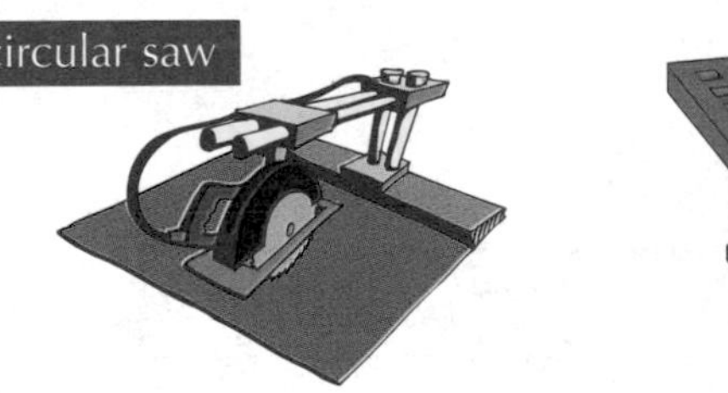

circular saw

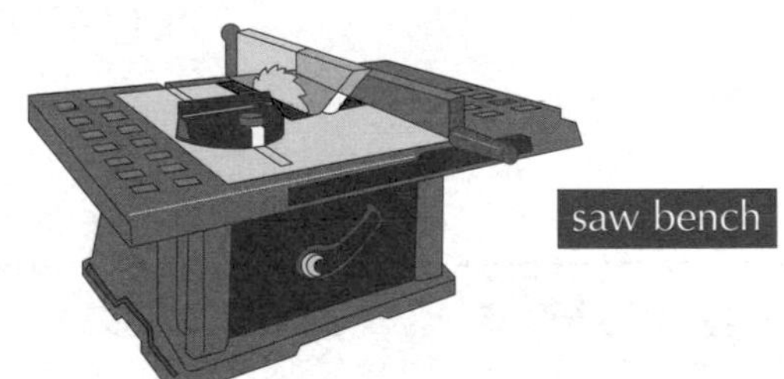

saw bench

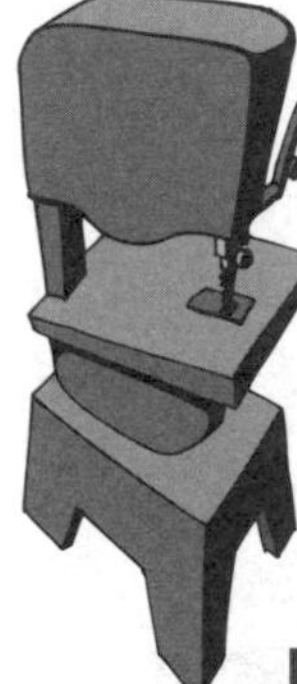

band saw

The band saw has a blade in a long flexible loop and is normally used to cut wood, but special blades can be bought for use on plastics and softer metals. The blades come in different widths and can be used for straight or curved cuts.

A Lathe is for making round things

Lathes come in two types — wood lathes and engineers' lathes (for working metal). A piece of material is held and rotated by the lathe, while the turning tool or cutting bit is pressed onto the material to cut it. Lathes are mostly used to produce cylindrical objects.

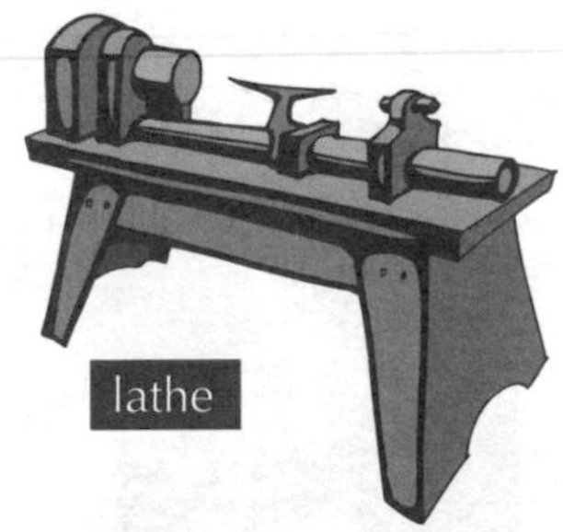

lathe

BIG machines — don't forget your safety gear

Once you've learnt the terms on the page, it's worth taking note of the safety precautions that need to be taken when using machines like this. For your own safety and for the exam.

Machine Tools

Planers, thicknessers** and **pillar drills** — for **cutting** and **drilling

1) A planer and thicknesser (either separate or both in a single machine) are used for flattening the surface of pieces of wood and for reducing their thickness to a specified measurement.

planer and thicknesser

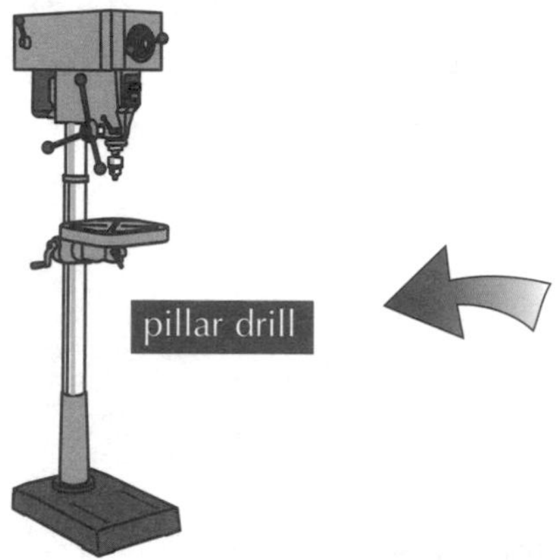

pillar drill

2) A pillar drill or pedestal drill is used with HHS twist bits, or other types of suitable bit (see page 14), to make round holes. They can be used on all kinds of materials, depending on the bit used.

Sanders** and **grinders** are mainly used for **finishing

Sanding disc

1) This spins a disc of abrasive paper which the material is pushed against.
2) It's used for trimming accurately to a line.
3) Different types of abrasive are available for use on wood, metal and plastics.

Bench grinder

1) This contains abrasive wheels of different grades (coarse to smooth).
2) It's used to remove metal for shaping or finishing purposes, as well as for sharpening edged tools such as chisels.

Milling machine

1) This is used to remove metal one thin layer at a time to produce the required size or shape.
2) It can also be used to make a surface absolutely flat.
3) It can produce a very accurate finish.

Have a look at some of these machines in the workshop at school

Machine tools have several advantages over hand tools — the work's easier, and more accurate. Imagine trying to get a surface absolutely flat without the help of a milling machine.

Hand-Held Power Tools

Power tools combine the advantages of machine tools with the convenience of hand tools — they're powerful and portable.

For example, a hand held power drill can be used to drill holes in a stone wall. The task would be too hard to do with a hand drill and you couldn't use a pillar drill because you can't move a stone wall into a workshop.

Power tools are hand-held motorised tools

In addition to the power drill, there are a few other power tools that you need to know about:

Jigsaws are for curved cuts

1) A **jigsaw** has interchangeable blades and variable speeds.
2) You can make straight or curved cuts in all materials, but it is quite slow.

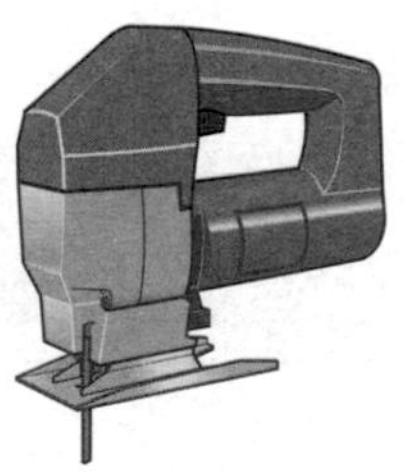

Circular saws are for straight cuts

1) You can get a hand-held version of the **circular saw** (see page 15).
2) In this case the wood is held stationary and the saw is moved along it, using adjustable fences for guidance.
3) It's good for making straight cuts very quickly in wood.

Power planers are for rough shaping

1) A **planer** is used like a bench plane to remove shavings of wood. It's used either to reduce the material to the required size, or for rough shaping.
2) The advantage of a power planer is that it takes much less effort and is much faster — but it's not as accurate as a bench plane.

Know your portable power tools from your fixed machine tools

These machines all have different uses and a couple of them come elsewhere in the book. Learn what they all do now and you'll find them much easier to deal with later on.

Warm-Up and Worked Exam Questions

Take a deep breath and go through these warm-up questions one by one.
If you don't know these basic facts there's no way you'll cope with the exam questions.

Warm-up Questions

1) Which of these tools are hand tools, and which are machine tools?
   tenon saw, thicknesser, bradawl, band saw, pillar drill, gouge, lathe
2) Draw two types of saw, and say what material(s) they would be used to cut.
3) What hand tool would you use to shave off thin layers of wood?
4) Give three safety measures that you should take when using machine tools.
5) Describe what a bench grinder is.
6) What's the difference between a jigsaw and a circular saw?

There's no better preparation for exam questions than doing, err practice exam questions.
Hang on, what's this I see...

Worked Exam Question

1 The diagram below shows a piece of metal which is to be made into the shape on the right.

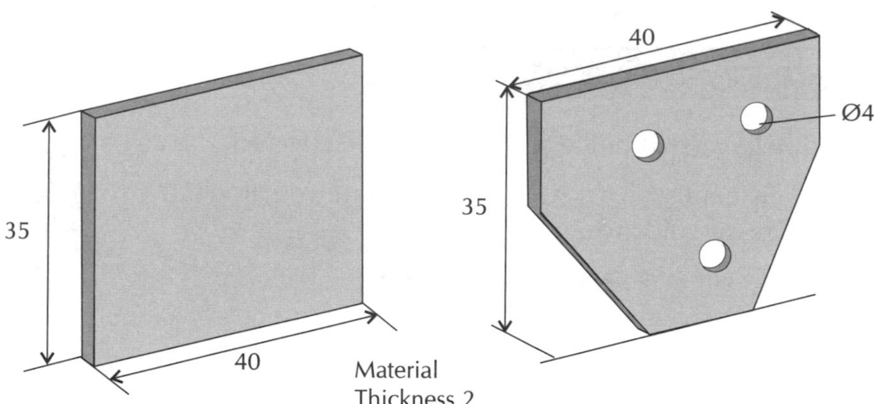

What tool should be used to do these things:

Make sure you think about the material being sawn — here it's metal, not wood

(a) Saw off the waste material.

Hacksaw

(1 mark)

(b) Smooth the edges.

File

(1 mark)

"Pillar drill" would also be suitable

(c) Drill the holes.

Hand drill

(1 mark)

Exam Questions

2 Complete the table below, to show the name and use of each tool.
The first one has been done for you.

Diagram of tool	Use	Name of tool
	Cutting metal and plastic	Hacksaw

(12 marks)

Deforming

Deforming means changing the shape of a material.

Most metals need to be **heated** before **bending**

1) Some thin pieces of metal can be bent cold on a jig or former.
2) Thicker or harder (ferrous) metals (see page 45) have to be brought to red heat in order to bend them. Non-ferrous metals have to be taken to their annealing temperature first (see page 46), and allowed to cool before bending.
3) This makes them soft enough to bend more easily, but the annealing process might have to be repeated as bending makes them go hard again ('work hardening').

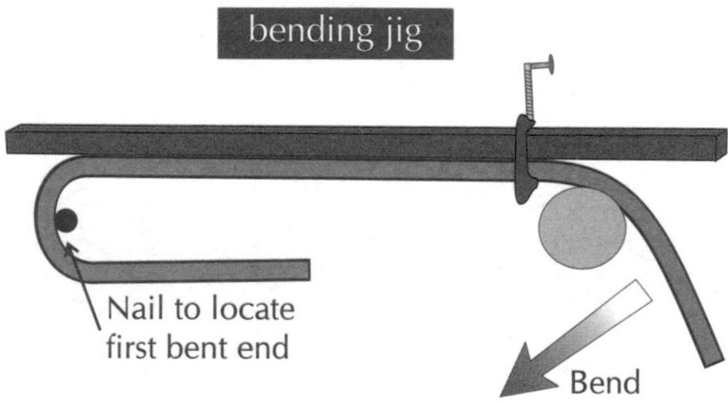

Sheet metals can be **folded** using a **sheet metal folder**

1) This is a method of shaping sheet metals such as aluminium and tin plate.
2) The outline of the product, e.g. a box, is marked out and cut from a flat sheet of metal.
3) The sides are then bent or folded up using folding bars, formers and mallets.
4) The corners are then joined using rivets, soldering or brazing.

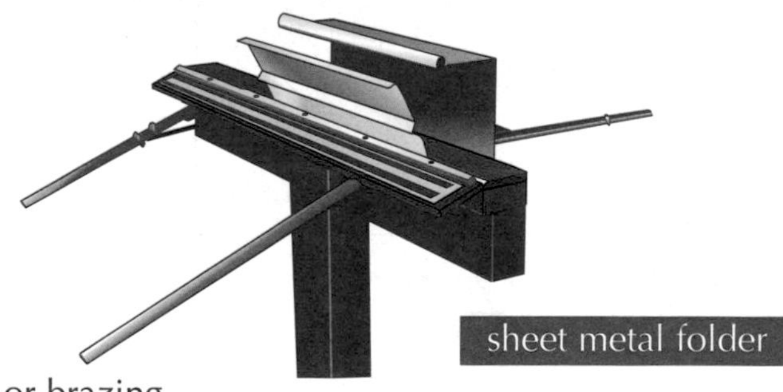

Plastics can be folded too — using a **line bender**

1) Line bending is ideal for use with acrylic sheets — e.g. for making picture frames and pencil holders.
2) With the bend-line softened on a strip heater (see drawing), the required bend can be made by hand, or by using a suitable jig.

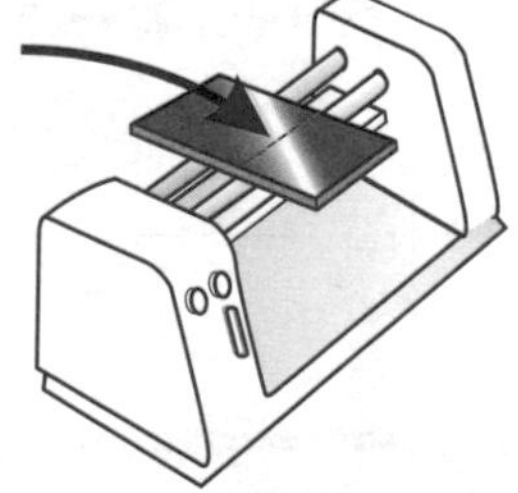

The element heats the plastic along the line where you want to bend it.

Learn the three main ways of bending

You need to understand what deforming means. After that, there's not too much to get through on this page — just three simple methods of deforming. Make sure you learn all the details.

Deforming

Laminating is *gluing thin strips* of wood together

1) Thin strips of wood (usually 2-6 mm thick) are glued together, like plywood.
2) This 'sandwich' is held in a jig, which keeps it in the shape of the finished product while the glue dries.
3) Items produced this way include chair and table legs, roof beams and rocking chair runners.

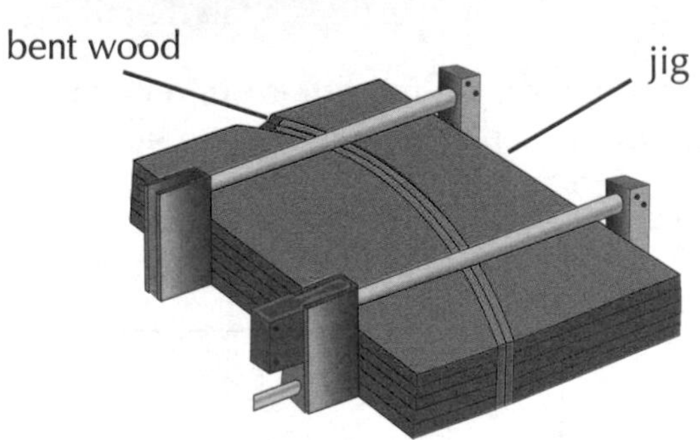

Iron and *steel* are *forged*

1) Metal, especially iron and steel, can be heated in a forge. A forge is a fire with air blown into the middle of it to produce a very hot flame.
2) When the metal's hot enough to have softened sufficiently, it's taken out and hammered into shape on an anvil.

an anvil

Press moulding is used to shape *thermosetting plastics*

1) A 'slug' of thermosetting plastic powder is put into a 'female' mould.
2) A former is pressed onto it and pushes the plastic into the mould.
3) Very high temperatures and pressures liquify the powder, and the plastic is set into a permanent shape.

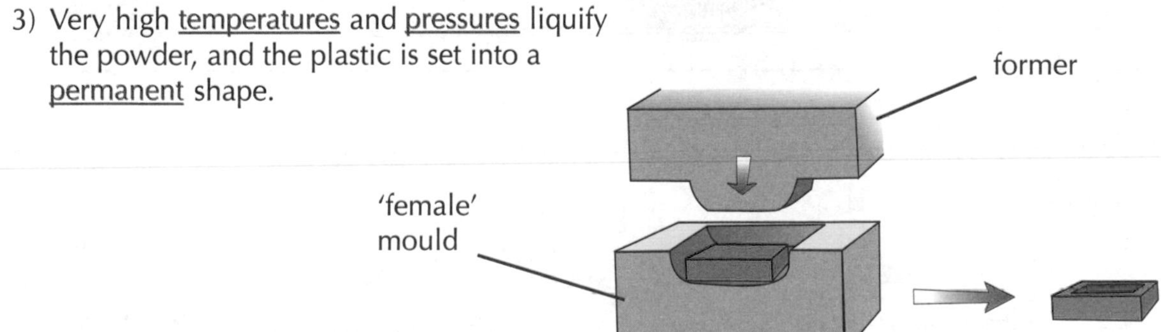

Always take precautions when you're using processes involving heat

These processes are all very different. Make sure you learn which materials you use each one for, and what kinds of things you can make with them.

Deforming

In vacuum forming, air is sucked from round the mould

1) A sheet of thermoplastic is heated until it goes soft.
2) A pattern (or male mould) is put onto the vacuum bed. The bed is then lifted close to the heated plastic.
3) The air is sucked out from under the plastic. Atmospheric pressure forces the plastic onto the pattern mould.

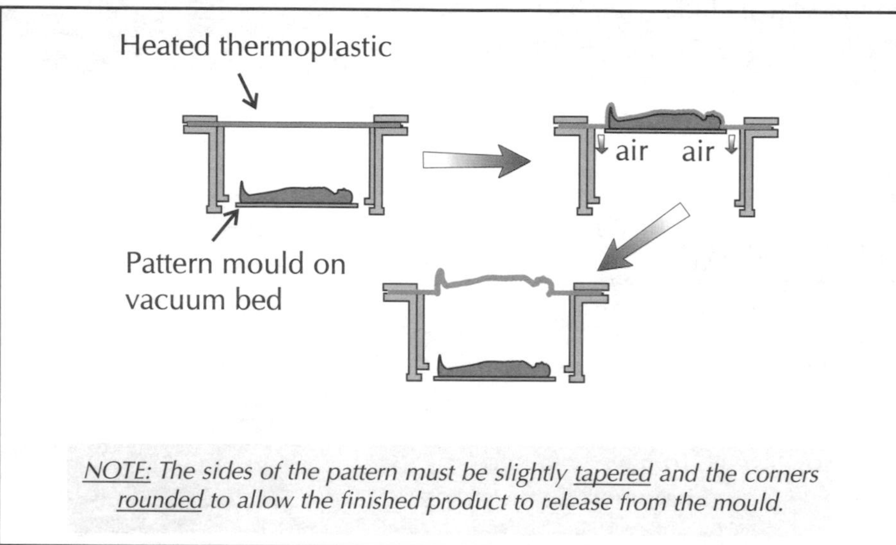

NOTE: The sides of the pattern must be slightly tapered and the corners rounded to allow the finished product to release from the mould.

Blow moulding uses air to blow plastic into a solid mould

1) A sheet of thermoplastic is clamped to the bed of the former and is heated until soft.
2) Air is blown under it, which forces the plastic up through a large hole in the bed.
3) This forms a bubble or dome, and is used to make dome-shaped products.

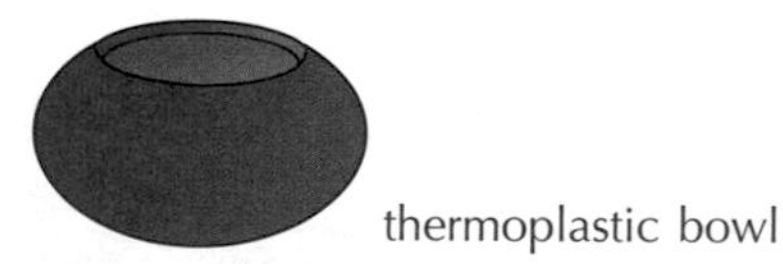

thermoplastic bowl

A more versatile method is where the softened plastic sheet is blown into a solid mould:

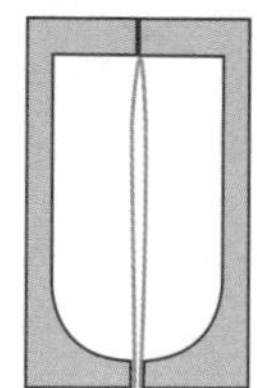

The plastic takes the shape of the inside of the mould...

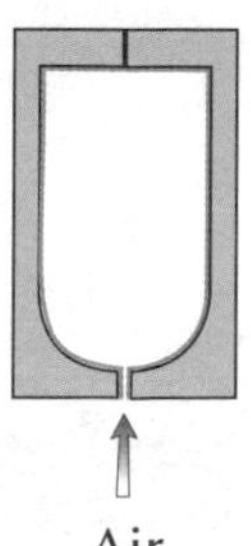

...which is then opened to remove the product.

This method is often used to produce bottles and containers.

Vacuum moulding and blow moulding do just what you'd expect

Pretty straightforward — vacuum forming works by creating a vacuum and blow moulding works by blowing air into the plastic. Learn the diagram and an example for both.

Reforming

Reforming is where metals or plastics are liquified, usually by heat and pressure, and then shaped in some form of mould.

Die casting is used to mould metals and thermoplastics

1) Die casting is a process used to mould metals and thermoplastics.
2) The material is melted and poured into a mould that is in the shape of the product.
3) Some plastic resins can be cold-poured into moulds (without heating). They harden or set through a chemical reaction.

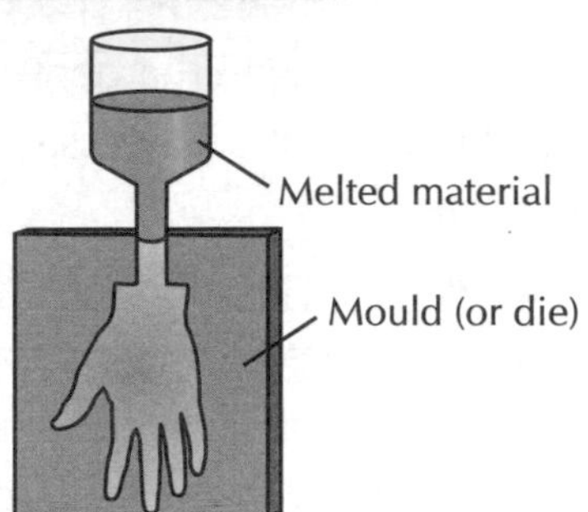

Injection moulding uses pressure to mould plastics

1) This is similar to casting, but the molten material is forced into a closed mould under pressure.
2) The plastic is often melted using built-in heaters.
3) This is an industrial process which is usually automatic and continuous.

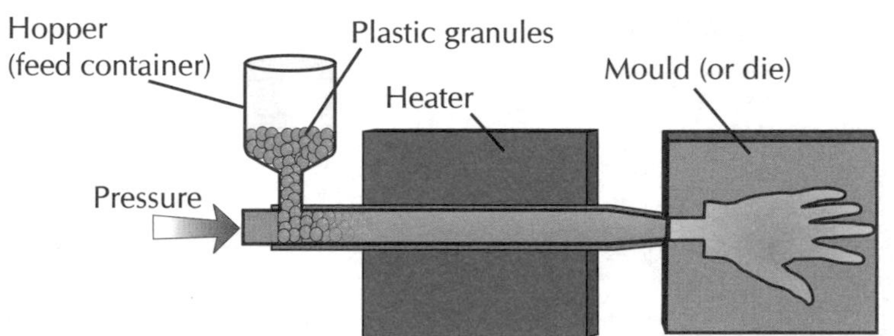

This is how they make those plastic models they sometimes put in cereal packs.

Extrusion produces long, continuous strips

1) Used for some metals and thermoplastics, this process is very similar to injection moulding.
2) The material is melted and forced under pressure through a die.
3) It produces long, continuous strips of the moulding in the shape of the exit hole. It's used to make plastic-covered wire, and plastic and aluminium edgings.

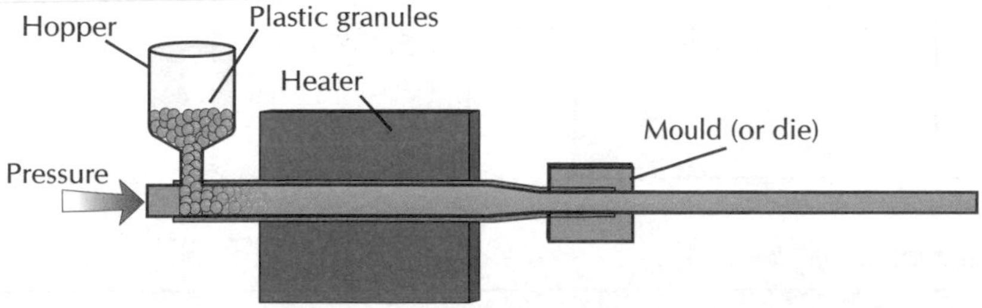

A 'die' is just another name for a mould

Reforming processes are usually industrial processes for mass production, and are not usually economically viable for small quantities of products.

Warm-Up and Worked Exam Questions

Doing these warm-up questions will let you soon find out if you've got the basic facts straight. If not, you'll really struggle — so take the time to go back over the bits you don't know.

Warm-up Questions

1) Explain the terms 'deforming' and 'reforming', in the context of resistant materials.
2) What is 'work hardening'?
3) Describe the process of laminating.
4) What is a forge?
5) Describe the process of press moulding.
6) How does blow moulding work, and what shape is produced in this process?
7) Explain the difference between die casting and injection moulding.
8) What type of shapes are produced by extrusion?

Worked Exam Question

Another worked question with hints to explain how to do it.
You'll get most out of them if you cover the answers and try them yourself first.

1 A plastic door knob is to be made from plastic resin.
It will be produced in quantities of 500, using die casting.

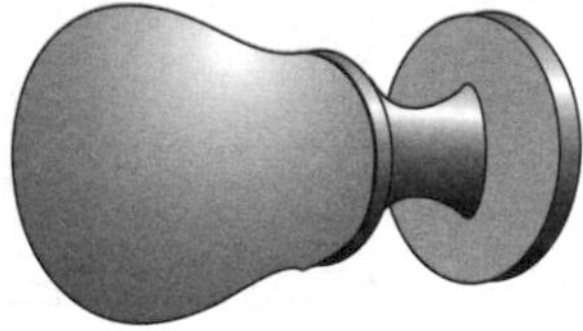

Fill in the diagram below, to show the main steps of die casting. The first stage has been filled in for you.

You get 1 mark for each stage and 1 extra mark for getting them in the right order.

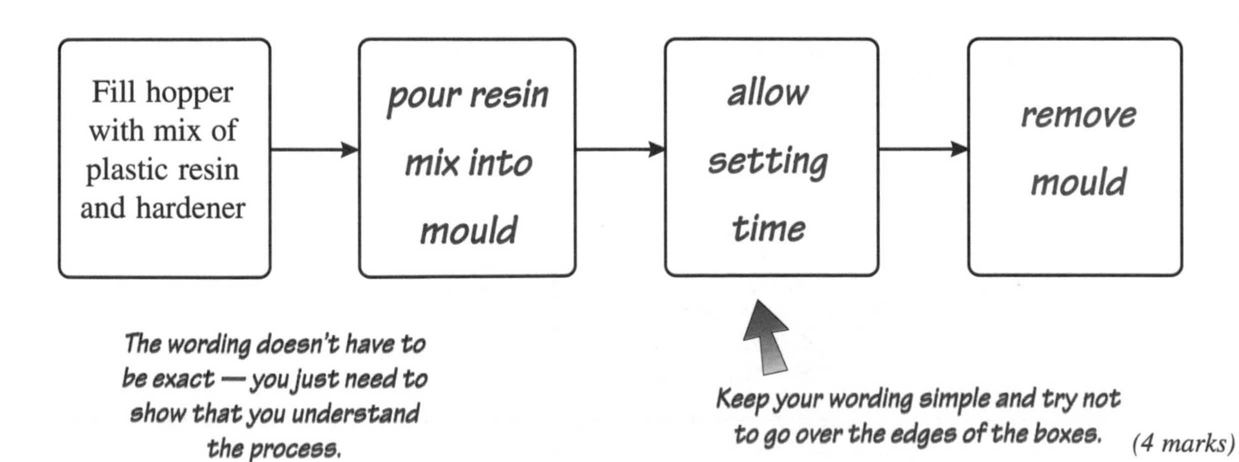

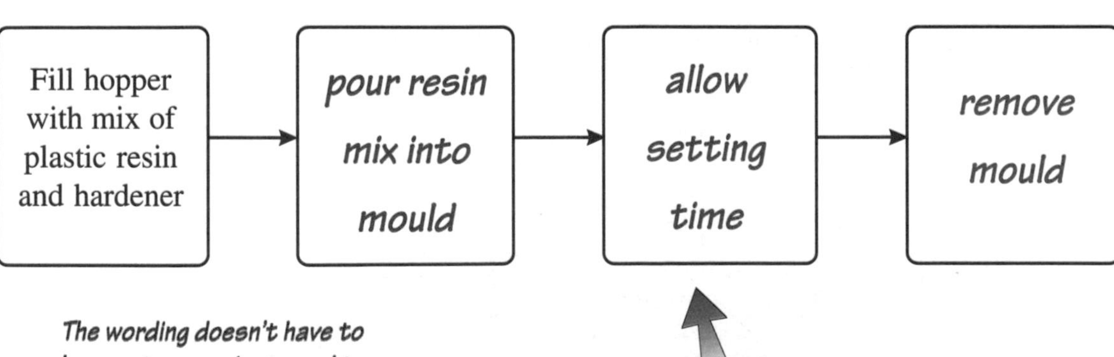

The wording doesn't have to be exact — you just need to show that you understand the process.

Keep your wording simple and try not to go over the edges of the boxes.

(4 marks)

Exam Questions

2 The diagram below shows a book stand.

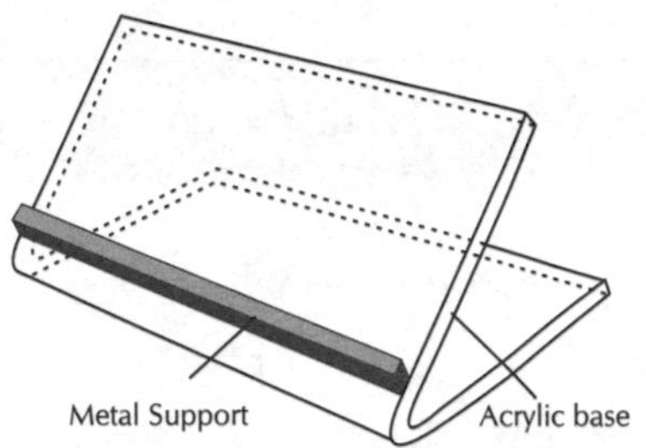

The book stand is made by bending a piece of acrylic into shape.
Name a machine that could be used for this.

....

(1 mark)

3 (a) This plant tray is to be vacuum formed.

Other than acrylic, what would be a suitable material to use?

....

(1 mark)

(b) The diagram below shows a section through a vacuum forming machine.
Complete the diagram, with labels, to show how the machine would be set up for forming the plant tray.

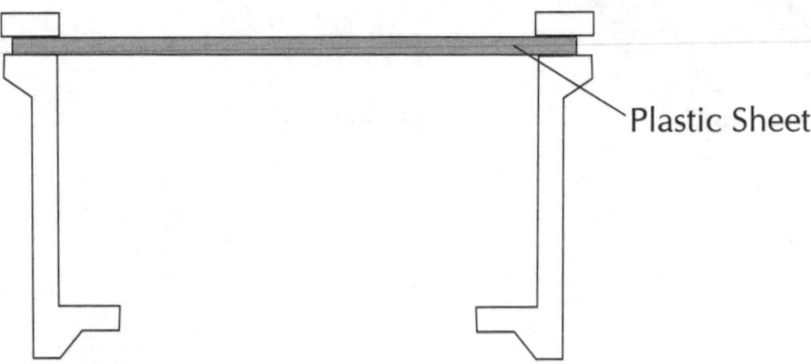

(3 marks)

Fabricating — Screws

Fabricating is the joining of pieces using the most appropriate method.
Different methods are used for different materials and in different situations.

Screws are used with woods, metals and plastics

1) There are different types of screws for use with wood, metals, and plastics.

2) Woodscrews often require 'pilot' and 'clearance' holes to be drilled before the screw is inserted. As the screw is turned by a screwdriver, the thread (the grooves around the outside of the screw) pulls it into the wood. Different types of head are available for different jobs, e.g. round, countersunk, slotted and cross heads.

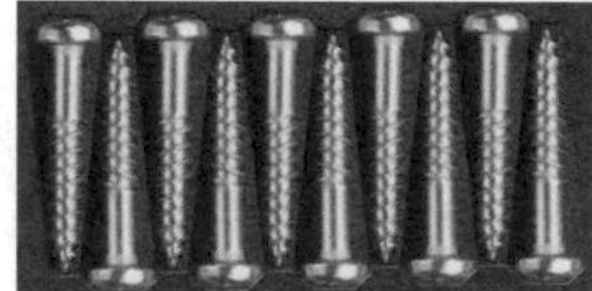

woodscrews

3) Self-tapping screws have hardened threads and are designed to cut their own threaded holes in hard materials such as (thin) metals and hard plastics. Even with hardened threads, self tapping screws should enter pilot holes the same size as their core diameter. (See next page for more on threading.)

self-tapping screws

4) Machine screws have a straight shank and are used with washers and nuts. Heads vary (round, pan, countersunk, etc.). Some are tightened with a screwdriver (cross and slotted types), and some with an Allen key.

screwdrivers

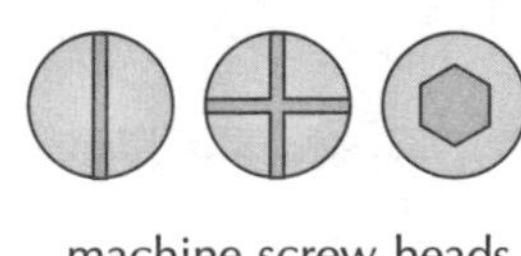

machine screw heads

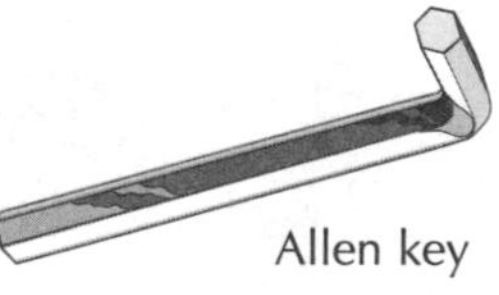

Allen key

Different types of screw have different functions

There are a few points to learn for each type of screw. Use diagrams of each to help you remember them. Bullet points are a good way of recording their different uses, and the materials they're used on.

Fabricating — Bolts and Threading

Bolts and threading are two more ways of fastening fabricated parts together securely.

Bolts are similar to screws, but tightened with a spanner

1) Bolts are similar to machine screws but have a square or hexagonal head and are tightened with spanners. Again, they are used with washers and nuts.
2) Screws and bolts are usually made from steel, brass or stainless steel, and are 'self-finished' or plated with zinc, brass, chrome, or black japan (a black varnish).

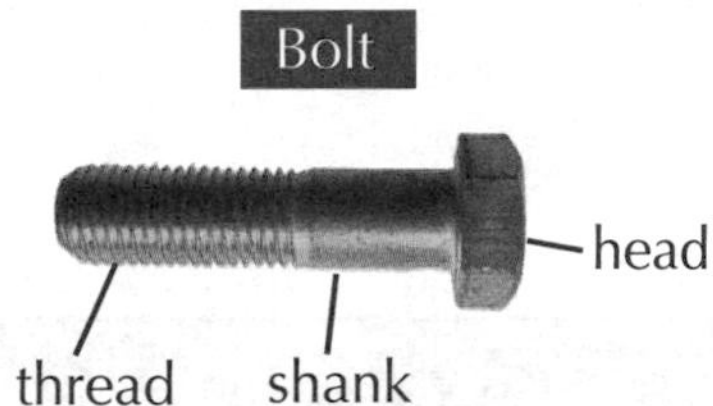

Threading is often used to make joints more secure

1) Threading is a method of fastening machine screws and bolts directly into a metal or plastic component without using nuts.
2) A hole is drilled and a set of 'taps' are used to cut a female thread in the hole. The screw is inserted into it and tightened until it stops.

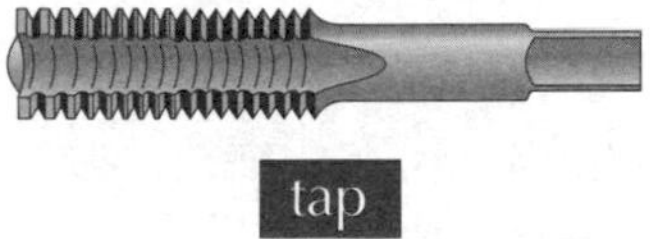

3) A round rod can be made to fit a threaded hole by cutting a male thread onto the outside of the rod. Male threads are cut either with a 'split die' or on a lathe. This allows components to be joined directly without the use of bolts or screws.

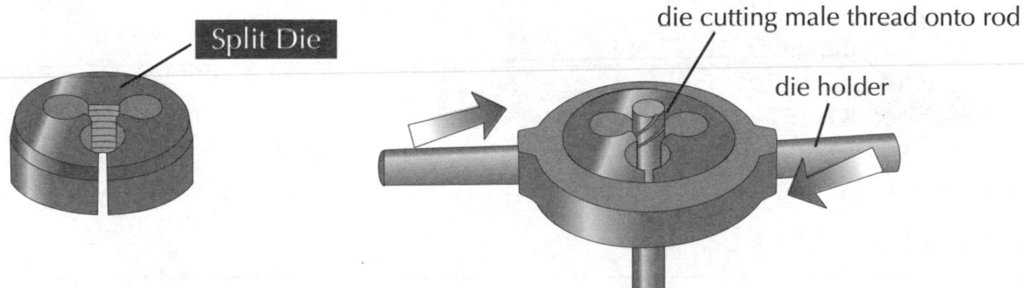

Threading is used to help secure bolts and screws

It's a good idea to make notes about these two methods of fabricating under separate headings. There's not too much to learn, but it's easy to get confused if you don't get them sorted out now.

Fabricating — Rivets

Rivets are used when you want to join pieces of sheet metal together.
There are two sorts you need to learn — rivets and pop rivets.

Rivets *are mainly used for joining* ***sheet metal***

1) A rivet is a metal peg with a head on one end. Rivets are used mostly for joining pieces of metal.
2) A hole is drilled through both pieces of metal and the rivet is inserted with a 'set' (hammer-like tool). The head is held against the metal whilst the other end is flattened and shaped into another head with a hammer.

standard rivets

Pop Rivets *can be used from just one side of the* ***metal***

'Pop' (or 'blind') rivets are now very common. They can be used where there is only access to one side of the material (hence 'blind' rivet). It's a fast and easy method of joining sheet metal.

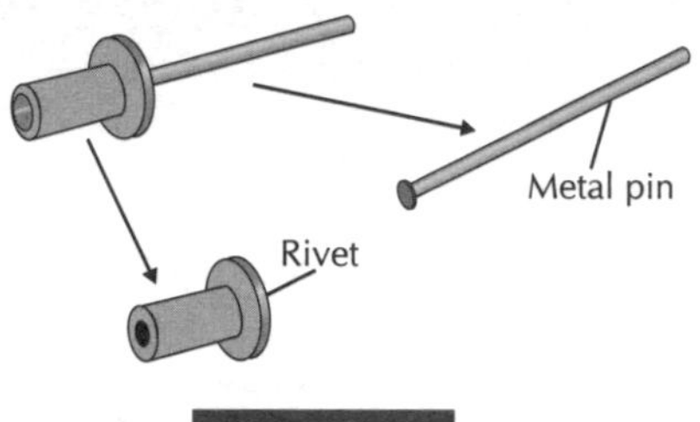

A pop rivet

How Pop Rivets Work...

1) Both rivet and pin are placed in the hole in the material.
2) The pin is pulled tight with a rivetter until it snaps off.
3) Pulling the pin tight causes the end of the rivet to expand and form a head on the other side.

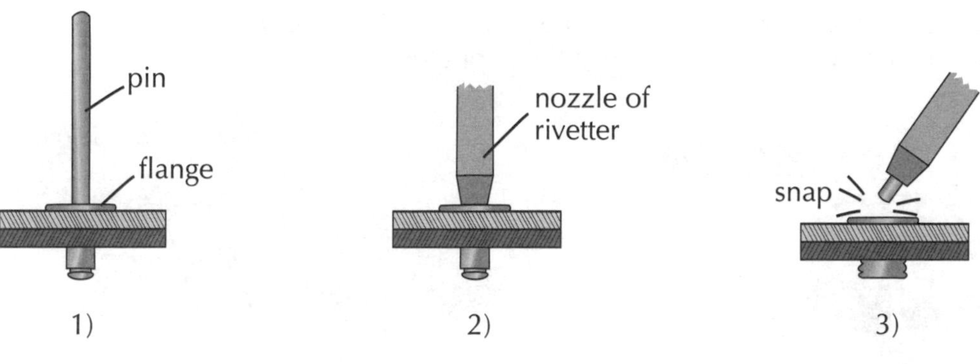

Rivets — used when you have access to both sides of the metal you're joining

And pop rivets are used when you can only get to one side. The best way of dealing with rivets is to break the topic into rivets and pop rivets. Use sketches to help you remember and describe them.

Fabricating — Nails and Adhesives

Nails are used for joining bits of **wood** together

1) These are similar in use to woodscrews but have a straight shank with no thread.
2) They're inserted with a hammer and can be punched below the surface with a nail punch to hide the head.
3) Nails are only used in wood and wooden boards, e.g. plywood. They're much quicker to use than screws, but the joint they make is nowhere near as strong.
4) Nails are mostly made from steel, but special ones can be made from other metals, e.g. brass for use in boat building. Like screws, they come with a variety of head and shank shapes for different uses.

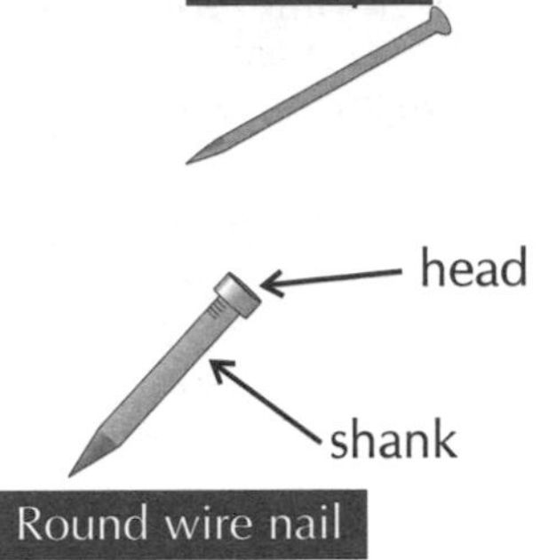

You need to **choose** the **right adhesive** for the job

1) There are many different types of adhesive for use with different materials and for different jobs, e.g. PVA and animal glue (for wood), contact adhesive and epoxy resin (for lots of materials).
2) Adhesives will only work properly if the right one is chosen for the job, and if the surfaces to be joined are thoroughly cleaned.
3) Some plastics can't be glued as they're too smooth, and have a greasy texture which stops the glue from 'keying in'.
4) Adhesives are often used to reinforce other methods of fabrication, e.g. joints in wood.

for more on adhesives see page 61

You often get a little tube of PVA wood glue with flat-pack furniture to reinforce joints.

The material you're working with affects what glue you use

When deciding which method of fabrication to use on a product, think carefully about which is more important — speed of assembly or strength. It's often a trade-off between the two.

Fabricating — Joints

Wood can be joined together in several ways — either by the traditional method of cutting joints and nailing and gluing together, or by using special fittings which can be taken apart again.

Some **joints** are **more permanent** than others

1) There are dozens of different joints, e.g. dovetail, mortise & tenon, housing, halving and mitre, for use in different situations. It's important to use the right joint in the right place.
2) Joints are often glued to make them secure and permanent.
3) Marking out and cutting joints takes a lot of skill. Accuracy is vital if the joint is to fit and hold together (as well as look good).

Joints with more **surface area** are **stronger**

DOWEL JOINT

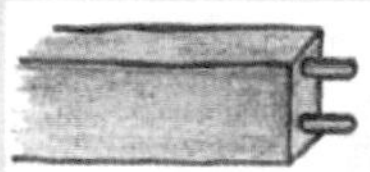

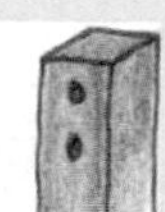

Dowel joints use a wooden or plastic peg, called a dowel, which fits into aligned holes to reinforce the joint. They often replace traditional joints in factory-made furniture.

MORTISE AND TENON

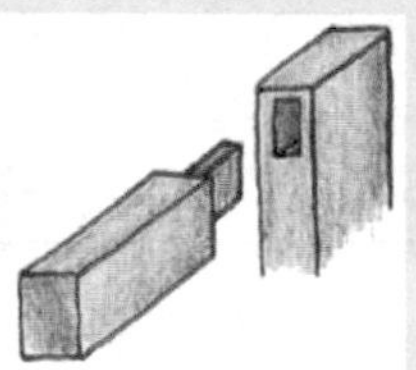

Mortise and tenon joints (cut with a tenon saw and mortise chisel) are really strong. They're often used in tables and chairs.

HOUSING JOINT

Housing joints are often used in shelving units as they provide a good surface area for gluing, and the shelf is supported all the way along its width.

DOVETAIL JOINT

Dovetail joints are very strong and look attractive. They're often used in drawer construction. They're very good but very difficult to make, unless you have a dovetail jig (see p113).

Which joint you use depends on...

a) whether you're a traditionalist, b) how much time you've got, c) your level of skill, d) whether you want to take the object apart again, e) how strong you want the joint to be.

Fabricating — Joints

Less secure joints aren't always a bad thing — they're often cheaper.

Less secure joints have their uses too

BUTT JOINT

It's pretty feeble but very quick and simple, and often used for joints in cheap pine furniture.

MITRE JOINT

Mitre joints are similar to butt joints but prettier and trickier to cut. Used for picture frames.

LAP JOINT

Lap joints have a larger surface area for gluing than butt joints, so they're a bit stronger. They're used in some drawers and boxes.

HALVING JOINT

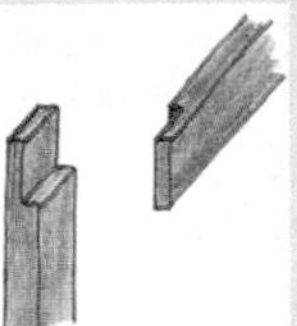

Halving joints are fairly strong — again, due to the large surface area for gluing. They're sometimes used in frame construction.

Knock-down fittings are non-permanent joints

1) These are blocks, brackets (plastic or metal) and other fittings which enable furniture to be assembled and taken apart again easily.
2) They are used instead of traditional joints, and are very fast to use, but are nowhere near as strong as glued joints.
3) Most types are assembled with screwdrivers or Allen keys.
4) They are usually used for cheap, 'flat-pack' furniture.

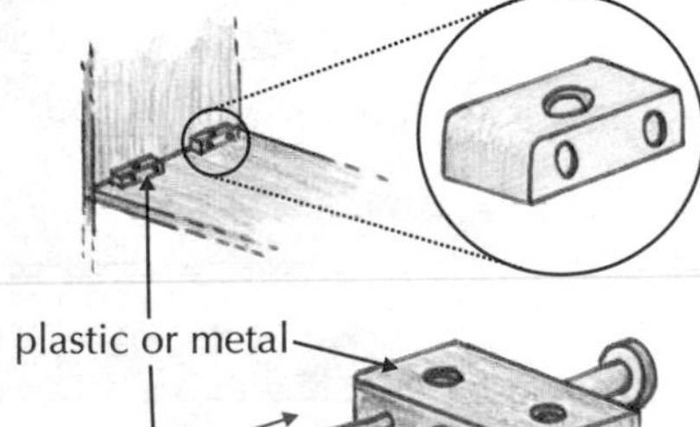

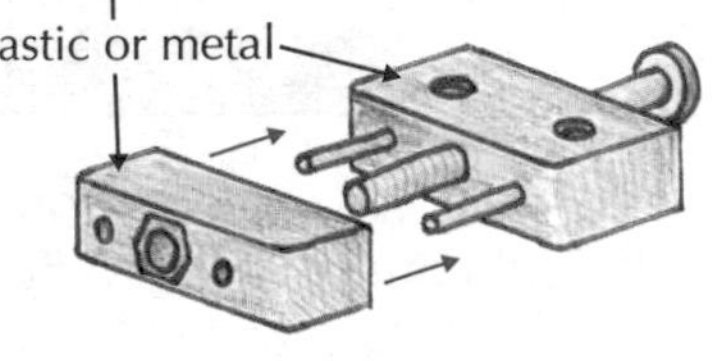

Learn the advantages and disadvantages of each of these joints

There are quite a few joints to learn, and quite a few odd names. You need to know the strength and shape of each one, as well as an example of what the joint is used for.

Fabricating — Joining Metals

You'll probably only need to use the first method of joining metals on this page while you're doing practical work at school. But you still need to know about the other two for the exam.

Soldering, brazing & welding are for joining metal

These are methods of joining metal by the use of varying amounts of heat.

1) Soldering is a relatively low temperature process. Solder, made from tin and lead, is melted onto the components to be joined, bonding them together when it cools and solidifies. A soldering iron or blow torch can be used for this process.

Soldering Iron

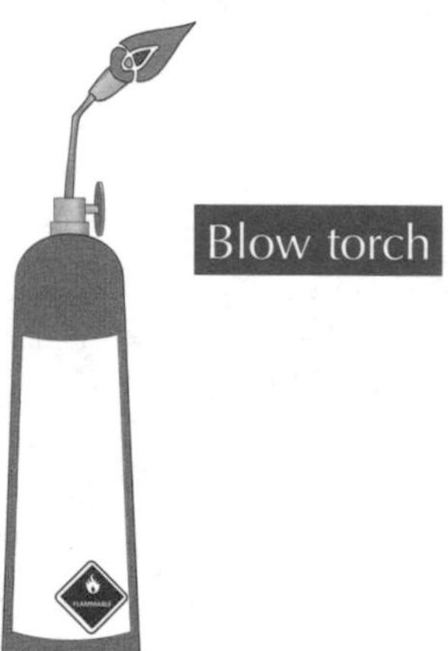

Blow torch

2) Brazing is a higher temperature process which uses brass spelter as the joining material. Either a gas brazing torch, a blow torch, or a brazing attachment for an electric-arc welder is used to heat the joint.

3) Welding uses a very high temperature from an oxyacetylene torch, an electric-arc welder or a TIG welder to actually melt the edges of the joint so that they flow together. Thinned metal or slight gaps are filled with metal from a welding rod. This is by far the strongest method of joining metal.

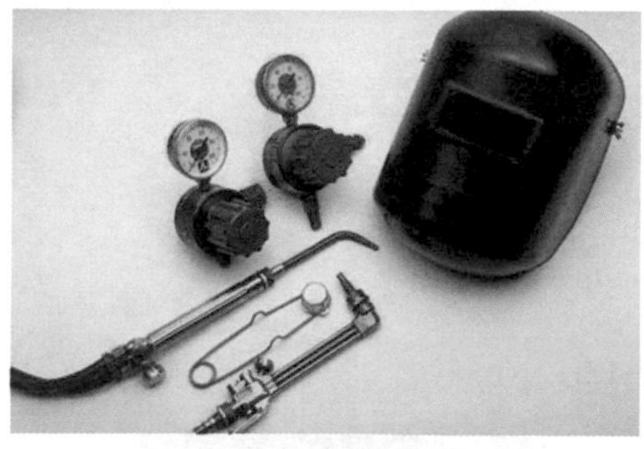

Welding equipment

The mask protects your face, particularly your eyes, from heat and sparks.

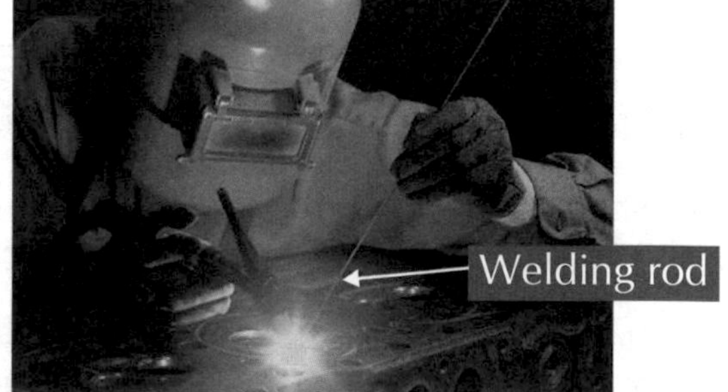

Welding rod

Different method = different temperature and different equipment

Extra care needs to be taken with heat processes.
Make sure you use the safety equipment provided and protective clothing.

Warm-up and Worked Exam Questions

Without a good warm-up you're likely to strain a brain cell or two. So take the time to run through these simple questions and get the basic facts straight before plunging into the exam questions.

Warm-up Questions

1) What is "black japan"?
2) In terms of screws and bolts, what do you use a tap for?
3) Name two ways to cut a male thread onto a round rod.
4) How does a pop rivet work?
5) Which is stronger, a mortise and tenon joint, or a dowel joint?
6) What are knock down fittings?
7) Briefly describe: soldering; brazing; welding.

Worked Exam Question

Remember, to get the most out of these, you should cover the answer and try them for yourself first...

1 The diagram below shows a wooden table.

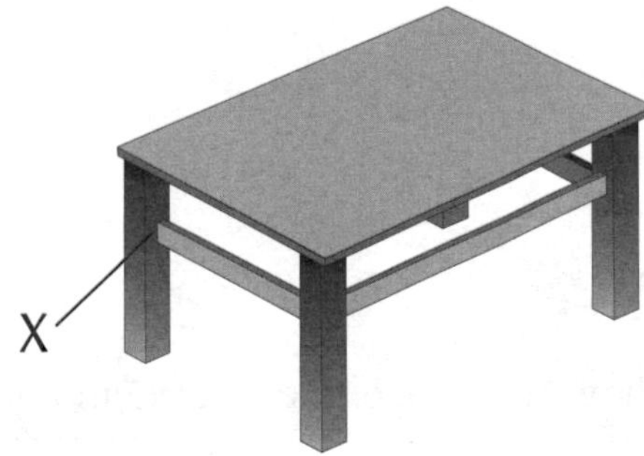

Any "suitable" joint will get the marks, so there's more than one right answer. But remember — it's got to be strong for a table.

Name and sketch a suitable joint for use at point X.

Mortise and tenon.

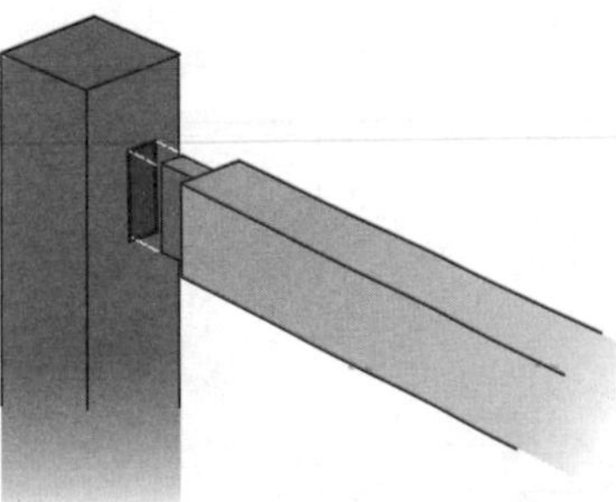

It's 1 mark for naming the joint, and 2 marks for the sketch.

(3 marks)

Exam Questions

2 The table below shows descriptions of four fasteners. Complete the table by writing the names of the fasteners next to the correct description. The first one has been done for you.

Description	Name
Threaded, straight shank. Hexagonal head. Used with washers and nuts.	Bolt
Tapered shank. Hardened thread. Cuts own threaded hole in metals and hard plastics.	
Straight shank. No thread. Used in wood. Inserted with a hammer.	
Tapered, threaded shank. Requires pilot and clearance holes. Used in wood only.	

(3 marks)

3 The diagram below shows the two elements of a pop rivet.

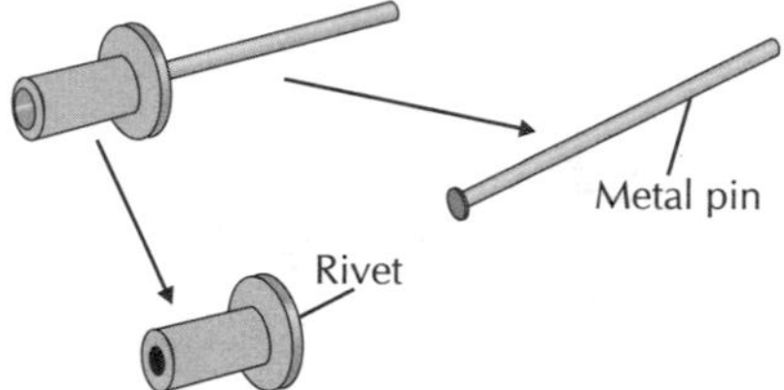

Complete the table below to show how a pop rivet is used to join two sheets of metal.

Step	1	2	3
Description	Pin and rivet are inserted into the hole.		
Sketch	pin flange		

(5 marks)

Fabricating — Preparing Joints & Assembly

*The joint needs to be **carefully prepared***

Before soldering, brazing or welding the joint needs to be carefully prepared.

1) Joints have to be well-fitting with minimal gaps.
2) They must also be very clean and free from grease. Fingerprints on the surface can stop solder or brass spelter from 'taking'.
3) 'Flux' has to be used when soldering and brazing and on some metals when welding. This stops the air oxidising the surface of the metal whilst heating it, as this too would stop the joint from taking.

Assembly** — putting the product **together

1) If permanent joining methods are to be used, it's vital to double-check the fit of the parts before final assembly. The project could be ruined if you can no longer get access to carry out other processes you might have forgotten.
2) Sometimes it is easier to clean up (e.g. with glasspaper) and apply a finish (e.g. paint) before final assembly, because access to inside areas for finishing is easier.
3) When gluing, soldering, brazing, or welding, it's vital to get the joint areas clean and free from dirt and oil.

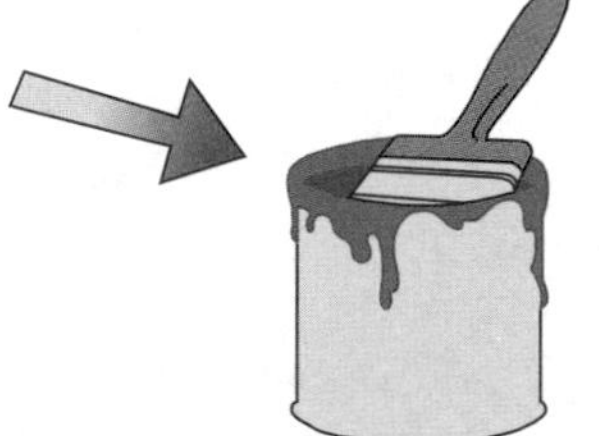

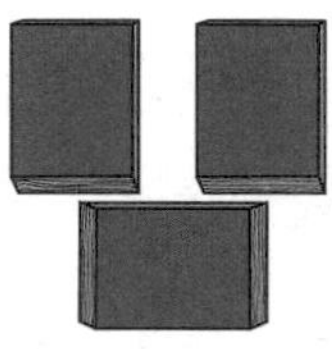

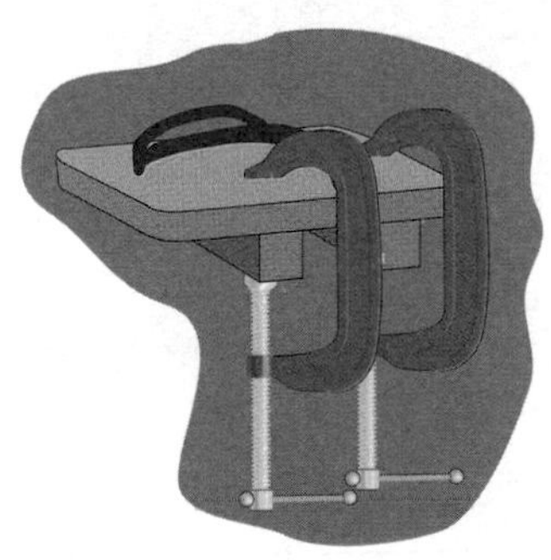

4) It's important not to touch areas to be joined after cleaning as fingerprints can leave enough grease on the surface to stop the joint from working.
5) When gluing, make sure you've tried the parts together first in a 'dry run'. This avoids getting halfway through gluing and finding that a part won't go on properly.
6) Gluing up (and often soldering, brazing and welding) needs clamps to hold the work securely whilst joining. Removing clamps too early can break the joint. Some glues require the joint to be clamped for 12 hours or more.

Final assembly needs to be done with a great deal of care...

Before starting assembly of your project think — have you completed all the necessary processes to the required standard first? You could ruin a lot of hard work if you start assembling your product too soon.

Finishing

There are several methods of finishing a product. Take note of the steps that need to be taken before you start the finishing process, and remember that different materials require different finishing processes.

Finishing — *protecting a product and making it look good*

Finishing is the final process in the making of any product.
It makes the product look good and protects it from moisture and dirt.

*Take steps **before** you start the finishing process*

Before finishes are applied it is important to remove any visible tool marks and blemishes with files, emery cloth and glasspaper.

*You can use **paints** to finish your product*

1) If paint of any type is to be applied, the surface must first be cleaned to remove grease and dust.

2) Different paints are produced for different materials and for use in different situations. It's important to select the correct type — otherwise it might not stick to the material, and it could even damage it. You've got to be especially careful when painting particular plastics.

*Paints can be used to give **distinctive** finishes*

Cellulose paint is generally applied to metal. It's sprayed on and looks great because it gives a very smooth finish. However, it's expensive as spraying means that much of the paint doesn't end up on the product.

There's more on finishing metal and wood on pages 47 & 51.

Finishing can dramatically affect the 'look' of the end product...

Failing to prepare a product before a finish is applied can prevent the finish from working properly. It can also mean that a product won't be sufficiently protected and won't resist wear and tear.

Warm-Up and Worked Exam Questions

You must be getting used to the routine by now — the warm up questions run over the basic facts, the worked examples help you with exam style questions, then you're on your own...

Warm-up Questions

1) In what way are fingerprints a problem in soldered, brazed and glued joints?
2) What device is used to hold materials securely whilst joining?
3) Why should you do a "dry run" before gluing parts together?
4) In the context of making a product, what is "finishing"?
5) What could you use to remove blemishes from metal before applying a finish?

Worked Exam Question

I'd like some hints, the answers written in — and a surprise. Two out of three's not bad.

1 The diagram below shows a joint between two wooden parts.

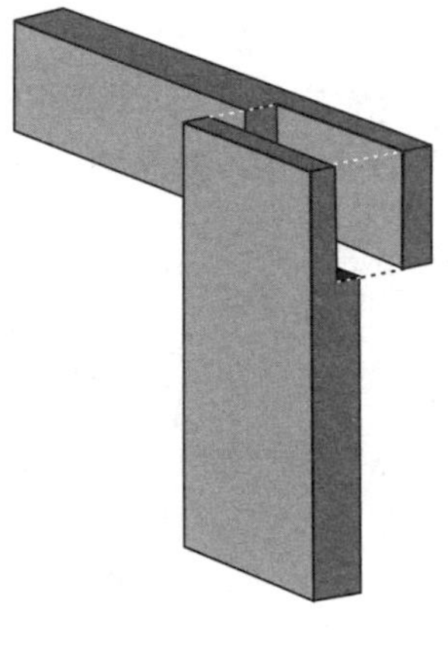

Look out for hints in the question, like this bit about it being clamped together.

Glue was applied to the joint, and the parts were clamped together.
When the clamps were removed, it was found that the joint had not stuck together.

Suggest **two** reasons why the joint might not have stuck.

1 *The joint might not have been clean.*

(1 mark)

2 *The clamps might have been removed too soon.*

(1 mark)

Exam Questions

2 The diagram below shows two metal parts which have been joined together.

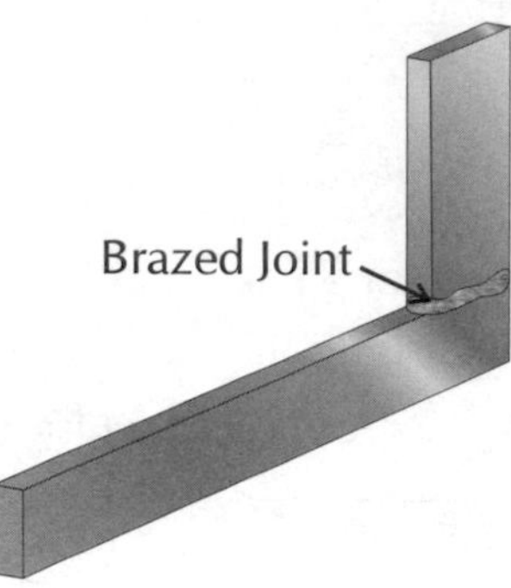

The metal parts were joined using the process of brazing.
During this process, flux was used.

(a) How does flux help to make a more effective joint?

....

(1 mark)

(b) After being joined together, the parts were painted.
The paint did not stick to the metal surface, and flaked off easily.

Assuming the metal was properly prepared,
suggest a reason why the paint might not have stuck.

....

(1 mark)

(c) The metal parts should have a smooth, brightly-coloured, painted finish.

(i) Name a suitable finish.

....

(1 mark)

(ii) How should the finish be applied?

....

(1 mark)

Computerised Production

Almost everything is designed on computer now — washing machines, hoovers, cars, planes, houses, cameras, computers. It's much easier and quicker than doing it all on paper.

CAD — Computer-Aided Design

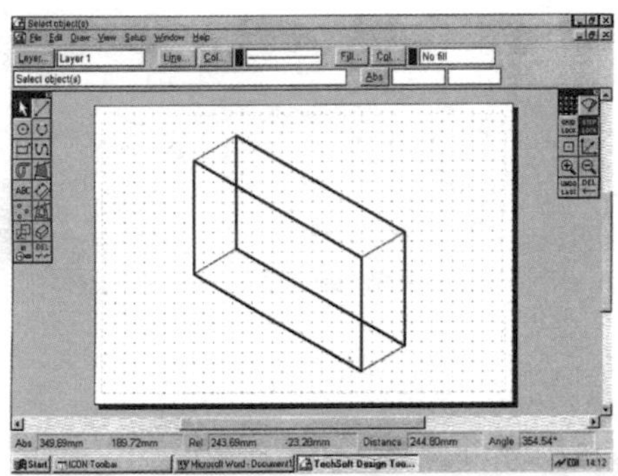

This is 'TECHSOFT DESIGN TOOLS — 2D DESIGN'.

1) Computer Aided Design involves designing products on a computer, rather than the traditional methods on paper.
2) Software ranges from 2D engineering drawing programs to 3D frame and solid modelling packages.
3) CAD allows designers to model and compare designs cheaply and relatively easily. Also, many problems can be ironed out before the production of prototypes.
4) In 3-D programs, finished products can be viewed from all angles, and scales of components can be worked out in relation to each other.
5) Finished drawings can be printed off on large format inkjet printers or plotters, or can be distributed electronically and instantly to production teams at factories across the world.

CAM — Computer-Aided Manufacture

a CNC milling machine

1) Computer-Aided Manufacture is usually linked with CAD.
2) Components and products are made on machines, such as milling machines, which are controlled and operated by computers rather than by people.
3) Products are designed with CAD software and control data is downloaded from the computer to the control unit of the machine.

CAD and CAM make production more efficient

This page is basically about how and why CAD and CAM have aided design and manufacture in industry. They've had a massive effect on the speed and accuracy of production — important stuff.

Computerised Production

Machines used in CAM are Computer Numerically Controlled — CNC

1) The machines used in the CAM process are Computer Numerically Controlled.

2) This means the CAD/CAM program works out the necessary movements of the tool head and sends the data to the machine in the form of numbers. The machine's onboard processor interprets the numbers and controls the movement of the tool head.

3) Machines which can be controlled in this way include lathes, milling machines and drilling machines.

a CNC cutter and plotter

CNC has advantages and disadvantages

ADVANTAGES of CNC:

1) Less cost due to less need for separate specialised machine tools for each product.
2) Less chance of human error.
3) The product can easily and quickly be changed without spending time and money retooling the machinery.

DISADVANTAGES of CNC:

1) High initial cost of the machines.
2) High cost of training programmers and operators.
3) Fast special purpose machines are cheaper than CNC machines for large-scale production runs.

CAD/CAM — when CAD and CAM are linked together

You'll need to know about the disadvantages of CAD/CAM, as well as the advantages. More terms are introduced on page 112, so make sure you know the ones on this page thoroughly before you move on.

Warm-Up and Worked Exam Questions

A short mini-section this time, but with an alarming number of three letter acronyms which, perhaps even more disturbingly, all begin with a C. Try these warm-up questions to check you've been listening.

Warm-up Questions

1) What does CAD stand for?
2) Briefly describe what CAD is.
3) What does CAM stand for?
4) What does CNC stand for?
5) Name a machine that can be controlled using CNC.

And now, the exam questions:
In the words of Darth Vader (a good friend of mine), "Do not under estimate the importance of practising exam-style questions in preparation for the Resistant Materials GCSE exam."

Worked Exam Question

1 A manufacturer is deciding on the most effective way of making their products. They can either use separate specialised machines for each product, or use Computer Numerically Controlled machines.

Describe one cost advantage, and one cost disadvantage of using Computer Numerically Controlled machines.

Advantage:

CNC machines can be cheaper, as you don't need to buy new machines to make different products. The same machine can be programmed to make different parts.

(2 marks)

There are 2 marks for each of these answers — so you need to give 2 marks worth of detail. The answer below gets 2 marks. You'd get 1 mark for an incomplete answer, like "CNC machines cost more."

Disadvantage:

To begin with, there is a cost disadvantage, as CNC machines usually cost more to buy than separate specialised machines.

(2 marks)

Exam Questions

2 Industrial design is often carried out using a computer. Describe how using Computer-aided design can be an advantage during the design process.

....

....

....

....

....

....

....

....

....

....

(5 marks)

3 A manufacturer wishes to produce a small number of round wooden door knobs. Describe briefly how the knobs could be made using computer design and production.

....

....

....

....

....

(3 marks)

Revision Summary for Section Two

Do as you did for Section One — try as many of these questions as you can and check back over the section to see if you got them right. It's a good way of finding out what you need to do more work on.

1) Define the terms 'deforming', 'reforming', 'fabricating', 'assembling' and 'finishing' in the context of resistant materials.
2) Name four different types of hand saw. What is each one used for?
3) Name three different types of drill bit. Say what each one is used for.
4) Describe a saw bench, and say what it is used for.
5) Describe how a band saw works.
6) Name two uses of a bench grinder.
7) Which power tool would you use to cut along a curved line?
8) What is 'work hardening'?
9) Describe the process of laminating.
10) What is a forge?
11) Describe the process of press moulding.
12) Draw a series of diagrams to illustrate vacuum forming.
13) How does blow moulding work, and what shape is produced in this process?
14) Explain the difference between die casting and injection moulding.
15) What shapes are produced by extrusion? Describe the process.
16) Name three things you must do before permanently assembling a product (using solder).
17) Give one advantage and one disadvantage of using cellulose paint.
18) Name the three main types of screw. How do they differ, and what are they used for?
19) Explain the difference between a bolt and a machine screw.
20) Name the tool used to cut a female thread.
21) Describe two different ways of cutting a male thread.
22) How does a pop rivet work?
23) Give one advantage and one disadvantage of using nails rather than woodscrews.
24) Why can some plastics not be glued?
25) Name four types of wood joint.
26) What is the main disadvantage of using dovetail joints?
27) What are knock-down fittings?
28) Describe the main differences between soldering, brazing and welding.
29) Why do you need to use flux when soldering and brazing? What does it do?
30) What do the abbreviations CAD, CAM and CNC stand for?
31) Give three advantages and three disadvantages of CNC over specialist machines.

Properties of Materials

Different materials have different physical and mechanical properties.

Mechanical properties are...

STRENGTH:

A material's strength is a measure of its ability to withstand forces without breaking. There are five main types of strength.

1) Tensile strength resists pulling forces — e.g. the rope in a tug-of-war.
2) Compressive strength resists squashing forces — e.g. bridge supports.
3) Bending strength resists forces trying to bend — e.g. surfboards.
4) Shear strength resists strong sliding forces — e.g. a rivet needs to withstand shear forces.
5) Torsional strength resists twisting forces — e.g. drill bits need to withstand twisting forces.

HARDNESS:

1) The ability to withstand abrasive wear and tear, denting and bending.
2) Very important for tools that cut, like files and drills.

BRITTLENESS:

1) Brittle materials can't withstand much stretching.
2) Brittle materials are more likely to crack or break than change their shape.
3) Glass and acrylic react like this under force.

DURABILITY:

1) If a product is durable it is able to withstand repeated use.
2) Durable products also withstand wear and tear, weathering and corrosive attack.

PLASTICITY:

1) If a product can change shape permanently, without breaking or cracking, it's said to have good plastic qualities.
2) This could mean that a material is malleable (changes shape under pressure so can be moulded, e.g. by hammering) or ductile (can be drawn into wires).

TOUGHNESS:

1) Tough is the opposite of brittle.
2) If a material is tough, it's hard to break or snap.
3) Armour and bulletproof vests need to be tough.

Not a difficult topic — but be careful of mixing the terms up

It's easy to get these five types of strength confused — so make sure you know these terms well before you go on to the next page. These are easy marks if you get them learnt now.

Metals

Some metals are pure metals and others (alloys) are mixtures of different metals.
Both types of metal can be classified into two basic groups — ferrous and non-ferrous.

*You can **buy** metals in **different shapes** and sizes*

1) Metal is extracted from the earth in the form of metal ore. It's then refined and processed to produce usable materials.

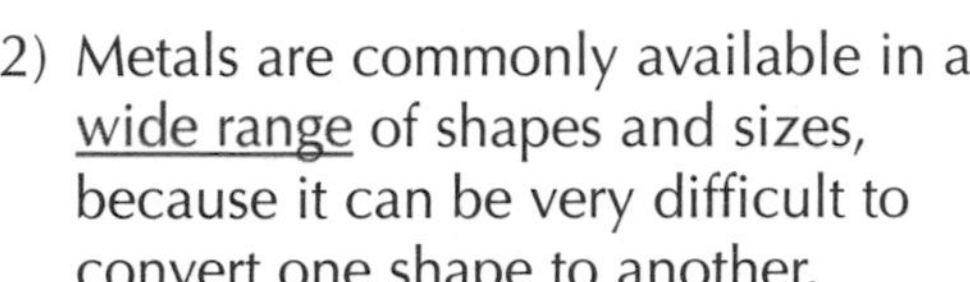

2) Metals are commonly available in a wide range of shapes and sizes, because it can be very difficult to convert one shape to another.

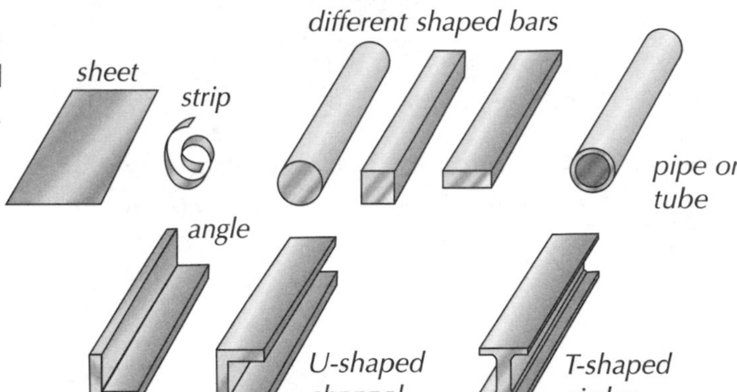

Ferrous** metals contain **iron

1) These are the metals that contain iron.
2) Because of this, almost all of them are magnetic.
3) Examples: mild steel, high-carbon steel, stainless steel

METAL	PROPERTIES	USES
MILD STEEL	Quite strong and cheap but rusts easily and can't be hardened or tempered.	car bodies, screws, nuts, bolts, nails, washing machines
HIGH-CARBON STEEL	Harder than mild steel and can be hardened and tempered. But it's not as easy to work and also rusts.	drills, files, chisels, saws
STAINLESS STEEL	Hard and won't rust, but is more expensive.	medical equipment, sinks, kettles, cutlery (e.g. knives)

***Non-ferrous** metals **don't** contain iron*

1) If a metal doesn't contain iron, it's non-ferrous.
2) Examples: aluminium, brass, copper

METAL	PROPERTIES	USES
ALUMINIUM	Lightweight and corrosion-resistant but expensive and not as strong as steel	aeroplanes, cans, ladders
BRASS	Quite strong, corrosion-resistant, malleable, ductile and looks good	door handles, electrical parts
COPPER	Relatively soft, malleable and ductile and a very good electrical conductor	wiring, pipes

Things to remember:

The two main groups of metals, examples of those metals, properties and uses. There are some good ways of prompting your memory, e.g. Stainless Steel — Sinks, Aluminium — Aeroplanes, Brass — B...

Metals

An **alloy** is a **mixture**, e.g. **brass = copper + zinc**

1) An alloy is a mixture of two or more metals, or a metal mixed with another element.
2) An alloy is a new material with different properties and different working characteristics.
3) Alloys can be grouped as ferrous *(contains iron), e.g. steel = iron + carbon*, and non-ferrous *(doesn't contain iron), e.g. brass = copper + zinc.*

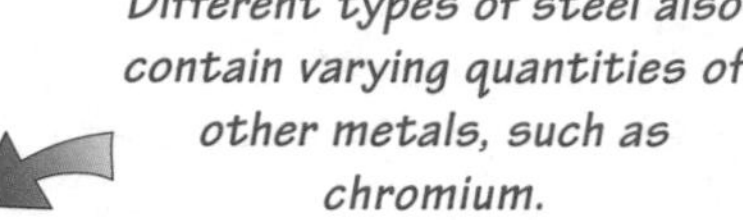

Different types of steel also contain varying quantities of other metals, such as chromium.

Heat treatments — for **softening** or **toughening**

Metals can be heat-treated to change their properties and characteristics. The three main types of treatment are listed below:

1) Annealing — softening metal by heating and leaving to cool.
2) Hardening — heating and rapidly cooling a metal.
   The metal is heated to its upper critical temperature then plunged into cold water. It leaves the metal brittle, so is often followed by a process known as tempering...
3) Tempering — to make the metal tougher and less likely to break.
   When steel is tempered, it's first cleaned to make it bright in appearance and then gently heated. As it gets hotter, it changes gradually from a pale straw colour to blue — and the colour shows you how tough it's become.

At the upper critical temperature, the atoms in the metal 'rearrange themselves' into a different structure.

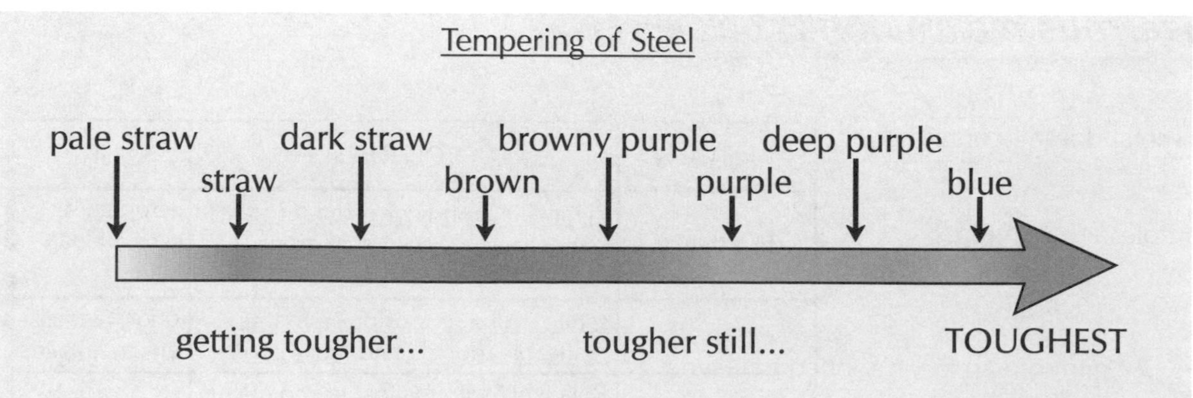

*Metals — heat treatment **changes** their properties*

Remember those examples: Pure metals e.g. iron, copper and zinc. Alloys e.g. brass and steel. Ferrous metals (contains iron) e.g. steel and.... iron. Non-ferrous metals — ABC — Aluminium, Brass, Copper.

Metals

You need to know about a few different kinds of surface finish.

Surface finishes — for protection and looks

Metals are rarely used in their raw form without treating them first. Most need some kind of surface finish — either for aesthetic (appearance) reasons or to provide protection.

1. PAINTING

A primer such as red oxide or zinc chromate is needed for steel (to form a chemical bond with the metal surface). Hammerite is a durable top coat that's available in a range of colours and finishes — it offers protection and is quick drying.

2. PLASTIC COATING

A metal is heated evenly in an oven and then plunged into fluidised powder (i.e. very fine powder that's made to act like a liquid by passing air through it during the process of dipping). The metal, with this thin coating of plastic, is then returned to the oven to completely fuse it to the surface.

3. POLISHING

This may be carried out by hand or by using a buffing wheel. The wheel is coated with abrasive polish and the metal is held against the spinning wheel until the required surface finish is achieved.

4. LACQUERING

This provides a barrier against tarnishing and oxidising, and is often used on decorative items such as jewellery. A thin layer of cellulose, gum or varnish is applied to leave a transparent coating.

Know the reasons for using finishes and all the different kinds

As with applying finishes to plastic and wood, metal must be prepared properly beforehand. The metal must be thoroughly cleaned (e.g. with paraffin or white spirit) before adding a finish.

Plastics

Most plastics are produced by industry using water, oil (or coal or gas), air and salt. There are two families of plastics — thermoplastics and thermosetting plastics.

Thermoplastics — recyclable and bendy

1) Thermoplastics are recyclable.
2) They don't resist heat very well, so they can be ground down, melted and re-used — very important in today's society of increasing waste.
3) Thermoplastics are easily formed into shapes.
4) A moulded shape can be reheated and softened without changing its properties.
5) Examples of thermoplastics: acrylic, ABS, polystyrene and polyethylene (polythene).

Thermosetting plastics — non-recyclable and (usually) rigid

1) These types of plastic are non-recyclable.
2) They resist heat and fire so are often used for electrical fittings and pan handles.
3) These types of plastic undergo a chemical change when heated (unlike thermoplastics) to become hard and rigid. They're not used in schools very often.
4) Examples of thermosetting plastics: melamine-formaldehyde, polyester resin, epoxy resin and urea-formaldehyde.

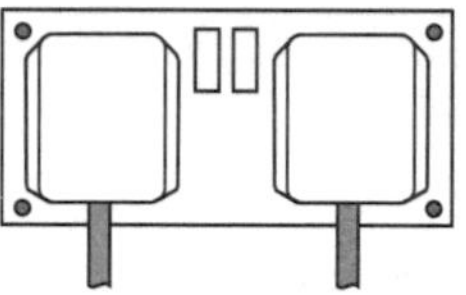

urea-formaldehyde

melamine-formaldehyde

Thermoplastics, thermosetting plastics — the key's in the name

Thermosetting plastics can't be remoulded — i.e. once they're set, they're set permanently and can't be recycled. Thermoplastics, in contrast, can be reshaped. Remember the benefits of each, and examples.

Plastics

There are a few other features of plastics you need to know about for the exam. It's important to learn about 'new' materials like the plastics below — they're a favourite exam topic.

Plastics come in a lot of **different forms...**

1. Plastics can be bought in many different forms — from powders, granules, pellets and liquids (pre-processed, for processing into finished products), through to films, sheets, rods, tubes and extruded mouldings (processed forms).

2. Plastics don't need protective surface finishes, due to high resistance to corrosion and decay.
3. But for a nice appearance, wet and dry paper (silicon carbide paper) is applied to remove scratches from the plastic, and followed up with a mild abrasive polish or anti-static cream.
4. Alternatively, a buffing machine can be used.

New plastics are still being **developed**

The following materials are fairly recently-developed and have lots of uses:

1) Plastizote is a closed-cell polyethylene foam that has eliminated the need for the toxic chemicals currently used in the foam industry. It's suitable for a wide range of products, including shoe insoles, buoyancy aids and reusable packaging.

2) Plastics that conduct electricity can be made by putting stainless steel fibres into plastics.

Make sure you know some examples of different forms of plastic

Plastic is used everywhere nowadays — it's versatile, resilient and convenient, and comes in lots of different forms. However, the extent to which it's used means that recycling plastics is a big issue.

Wood

Woods can be divided into two main categories — softwood and hardwood.
This is not a description of the wood — it just means what type of tree it comes from.

Softwood — evergreen trees, like pine

1) Most softwood trees are coniferous (cone bearing). They typically have thin needle-like leaves and are evergreen — e.g. pine, cedar and yew.
2) They grow in colder climates and are fast growing — most reaching maturity within 30 years. This makes them easy to replace with new trees, so they're usually cheaper than hardwoods.

Pines:

1) There are several types of pine but they're all generally pale yellow with brown streaks.
2) Scots pine is fairly strong but knotty.
3) Parana pine is more expensive — it's hard and is best used for interior joinery.

Pine trees — before and after the 'chop'.

Hardwood — deciduous trees, like oak

1) Most hardwood trees are broadleaved and deciduous (they shed their leaves annually) — e.g. oak, mahogany, beech and elm.
2) Broadleaf trees grow in warm climates and are usually slow growing. They can take around a hundred years to mature, so they're generally more expensive than softwoods.

A deciduous tree in autumn.

COLOURS OF THE COMMON HARDWOODS:

mahogany	reddish brown	elm	light reddish brown
beech	creamy/pinkish	oak	rich light brown

In Britain we get a mix of softwood and hardwood trees

Softwoods — coniferous, evergreen, fast growing, yellow and brown (pines), cheaper.
Hardwoods — broadleaves, deciduous, slow growing, tend to have a richer colour, more expensive.

Woodstains and Varnishes

Varnish is used to protect wood and enhance its appearance...

Most woods need protection, particularly if they're going to be used outdoors. Most hardwoods have an attractive grain that people want to display, so they often don't have paint as a surface finish.

1) Polyurethane varnish can be used to seal and protect the surface of the wood, and give it a smooth surface finish. You can buy it clear or in a wide range of colours.

Woodstains help to preserve the natural grain of wood

2) Woodstain can be applied to wood to enhance the appearance of the wood's grain. It's available in natural colours but also in bright blues, reds etc. Stains usually don't protect the wood, so varnish may need to be applied afterwards.

3) Oil can be used to maintain the natural appearance of the wood. Some oil-based finishes also offer protection to wood used outdoors.

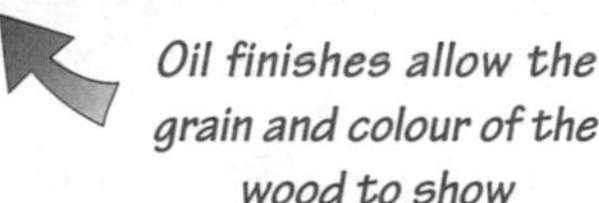

Oil finishes allow the grain and colour of the wood to show

Paint can protect and colour wood...

1) Paint is often used to colour and protect wood. Emulsion paints are cheap, but they are water-based, so they don't protect wood from water.

2) Polyurethane paint is more expensive but is waterproof and much tougher.

Applying a finish to wood serves two purposes...

Varnish, woodstain and oil can all be used to protect wood, as well as enhance the natural appearance of the wood. Certain paint can also be used to protect wood, and add colour.

Manufactured Boards

Solid woods (see p50) are cut straight from the tree. Man-made woods (boards) are made from the bits of waste that are produced when the trunks and branches are cut into planks.

Plywood — lots of layers of wood

Plywood is a very popular man-made board, used for building and general construction.

1) Plywood is very strong for its weight and thickness, compared with solid wood.
2) It's made up of several layers — always an odd number of them.
3) The layers are glued with their grain at 90 degrees to each other — which is why it's so strong.

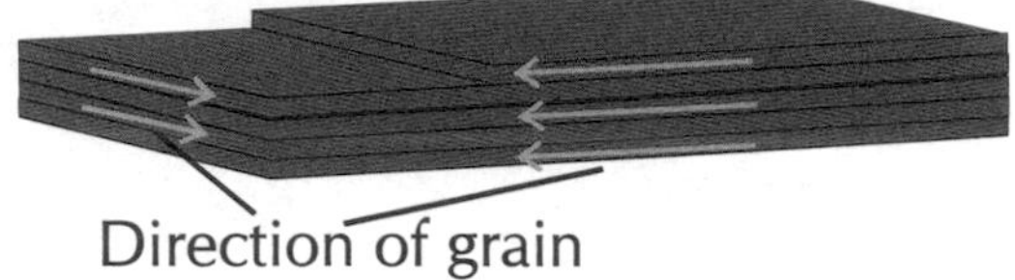

4) The outside of the board can be finished with a nice veneer (a thin layer of good quality wood) to make it look more attractive.

Blockboard and laminboard — blocks in a 'sandwich'

Blockboard and laminboard are boards of similar construction. Although not as strong as plywood, they're a cheap substitute, especially when thicker boards are required.

1) Strips of softwood are glued together, side by side, and sandwiched between two veneers. The veneers add strength and make the board look nicer.
2) The outer veneers are glued with their grain at right angles to the grain of the inner core — this makes the board stronger.
3) The softwood used is usually pine or spruce.
4) The width of the softwood for laminboard is between 5 mm and 7 mm.
5) The width of the softwood for blockboard is thicker, at between 7 mm and 25 mm.

Cross-section of blockboard/laminboard

Veneers

Strips of softwood

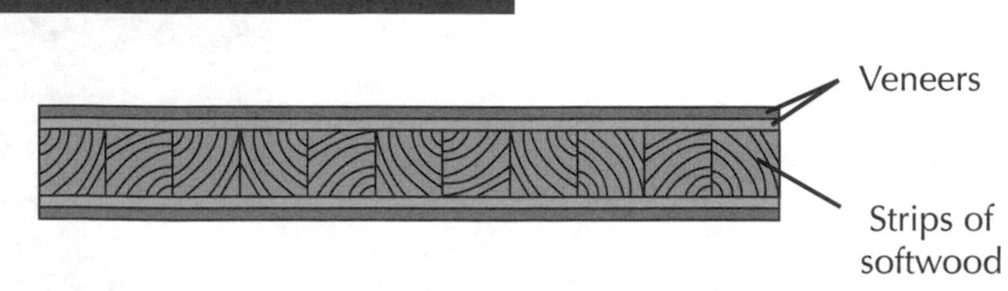

Attractive veneers can hide unattractive man-made board

Manufacturers use several tactics to strengthen man-made boards — adding layers of wood and angling the grain are both effective ways of improving strength and durability.

Manufactured Boards

MDF and chipboard are not particularly attractive materials. But they have their strengths — they're cheap and easy to use. Veneers and finishes can be used to strengthen them and improve their appearance.

MDF and chipboard are very cheap

MEDIUM DENSITY FIBREBOARD

1) Medium density fibreboard (MDF) is formed by compressing wood fibres under high temperatures.
2) It's a popular board that's very cost-effective and much cheaper than using solid wood.
3) MDF has smooth faces and takes paint and other finishes well.
4) MDF is easy to machine, but it's advisable to wear a mask when sawing it. There is a danger of inhaling the tiny wood fibres.
5) MDF is generally used to make interior products.

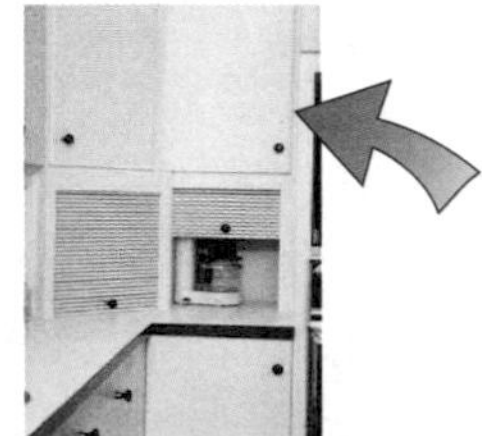

Painted MDF can be used to make kitchens and other domestic products

CHIPBOARD

1) This is produced by compressing particles of softwood with glue and heating them under high pressure.
2) It's cheap but not very strong, so is usually used with a hardwood or plastic veneered surface in cheap furniture.
3) Like MDF, it's generally used to make interior products.

Chipboard

Manufactured boards use up wood scraps — so they're cheap

Man-made boards are available in large sizes — because they're not restricted by the size of the tree, like solid wood is. Knock-down (KD) joints (see p31) are the easiest way to join these boards.

Composites

Composites and 'smart materials' have allowed new types of product to be made.

Composites — improved properties through bonding

1) When two or more materials are combined by bonding, a composite material is formed.
2) Mechanical and other properties are improved, resulting in excellent strength-to-weight ratios in the majority of composites.
3) Tufnol is an example of a composite: woven linen is impregnated with a phenolic resin. This can then be used in gears, bearings etc.

Plastic can be reinforced with glass or carbon fibres

GLASS-REINFORCED PLASTIC (GRP)

1) Glass-Reinforced Plastic (GRP) is a popular choice for large structural items such as boats and car bodies.
2) This reinforced plastic has glass fibre strands that give greater strength to the material.
3) The glass fibre is available as woven fabric, matting and loose strands.

CARBON FIBRE

1) This is similar to GRP, but instead of glass fibres, carbon fibres are used. This makes the material much stronger.
2) As well as being mechanically stronger, the material is also lighter in weight.
3) Products made from carbon-fibre composites include protective helmets, bulletproof vests and racing cars.

Composites — improve the properties of materials and products

Creating composite materials allows you to take the properties that you want from different materials. This can give you a new, 'improved' material that meets your needs.

Smart Materials

Scientists are continually developing ranges of new materials with new properties. Smart materials have been developed which change their properties in response to changes in their environment.

'Smart' materials have clever properties

NITINOL

1) Nitinol is a 'shape memory alloy', and is an example of a so-called 'smart material'.
2) It can be easily shaped when cool, but returns to a 'remembered' shape when heated above a certain temperature.
3) So if your glasses are made of this and you accidentally bend them, you can put them into a bowl of hot water and they'll go back into shape.

SILICON

1) Silicon is a semiconductor, meaning its resistance decreases as its temperature increases.
2) Single crystals of silicon are cut into thin wafers and have transistors (and other circuit elements) etched onto the surface. A large chip of 20cm diameter can contain up to one thousand million circuit elements.
3) Computers have their Central Processing Unit (CPU) made from a single integrated circuit (chip).

Integrated circuit

Silicon — a smart material of diverse uses

Smart materials have enabled manufacturers to improve existing products, as well as develop new ones. You need to know these examples well for the exam — they're an important area of research.

Warm-Up and Worked Exam Questions

Time to take well-deserved break. That was a long mini-section with more facts to learn about materials than can possibly be good for you. First of all, test yourself on the warm-up questions. Then have your best shot at the exam questions — you know the drill...

Warm-up Questions

1) What's the difference between toughness and hardness?
2) Name one ferrous alloy, and one non-ferrous alloy.
3) How can you harden a metal?
4) Describe the difference between thermoplastics and thermosetting plastics.
5) Which is generally cheaper, hardwood or softwood?
6) What is plywood?
7) Name three composite materials, and say what they're made of.

Worked Exam Question

1 The diagram below shows a box, designed for use outside in the garden.

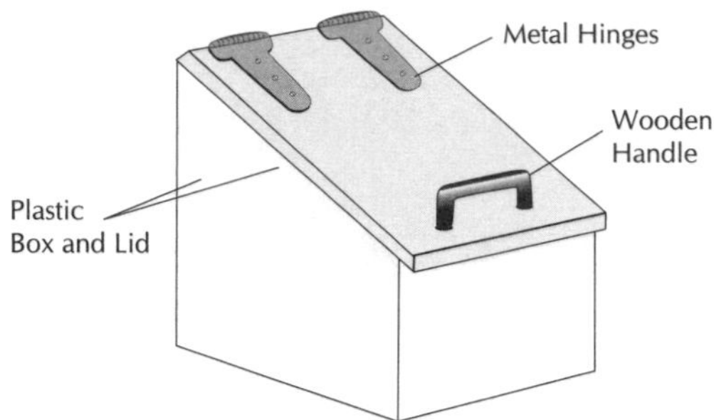

(a) Name a specific material that could be used to make each of these parts.

(i) Metal hinges: *Stainless steel* ....

(1 mark)

(ii) Plastic box: *Polystyrene* ....

(1 mark)

Think about the properties these parts need to have, e.g. the wood you choose needs to be hard and durable.

(iii) Wooden handle: *Oak* ....

(1 mark)

(b) For one of the materials named in part (a), explain one property that makes it a good material to use for this purpose.

Material:

Stainless steel ....

Property:

Stainless steel won't rust, which is important as the box is to be used outdoors. ....

(2 marks)

It's 1 mark for giving the property (won't rust), and 1 mark for saying why it's good for this purpose.

Exam Questions

2 Complete the table below by giving an example of an item / product where the property named is important. The first one has been done for you.

Property	Example
Bending strength	Shelf
Hardness	
Durability	
Compressive strength	
Toughness	
Shear strength	

(5 marks)

3 (a) The plastic pot shown below is to be produced using a vacuum forming process. Name a suitable material that it could be made out of.

Material: ....

(1 mark)

(b) The diagram below shows a saucepan handle. Name a suitable material that it could be made out of.

Material: ....

(1 mark)

Exam Questions

4 The diagram below shows a typical car.

The body of the car is made from separate metal panels.

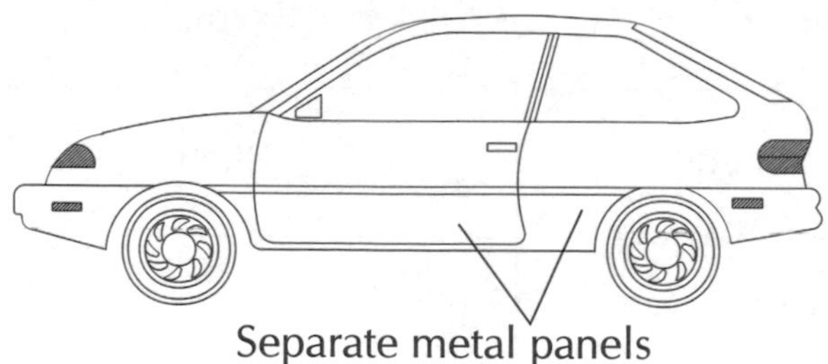

Car body panels are usually made from pressed mild steel or aluminium.

(a) Give two advantages of using aluminium instead of mild steel.

....

....

....

(2 marks)

(b) Despite the advantages of aluminium, mild steel is more commonly used to make car body panels. Give two advantages of using mild steel.

....

....

....

(2 marks)

(c) Formula One racing cars require body panels which are as strong and as lightweight as possible. Name and describe a suitable material for this purpose.

....

....

....

(2 marks)

Fixtures and Fittings

There are many fixtures and fittings available on the market.
You can use these for locking, hinging and joining.

There are **four** main types of **hinge**

Hinges are available in steel, brass and nylon, and can be coated to match a piece of furniture.
The part of the hinge that moves is called the knuckle.

1) Butt hinges are the most common type of hinge used for hanging doors.
2) The two parts of the hinge are set into the door and frame.
3) They're available in brass or steel.

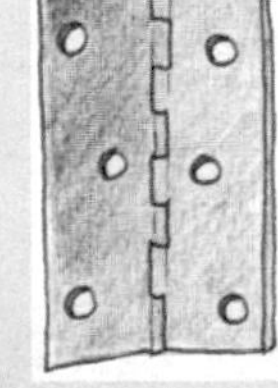

1) Flush hinges are screwed directly onto the surface of the wood, so they're easier to fit than butt hinges.
2) They're usually used for lightweight jobs.

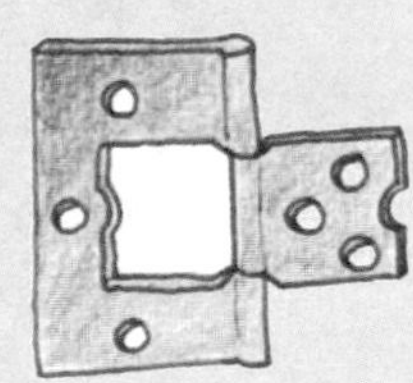

1) Tee hinges are often used outside — for things like shed doors or garden gates. The longer 'strap' allows the hinge to support a greater weight.
2) They're often covered in black enamel.

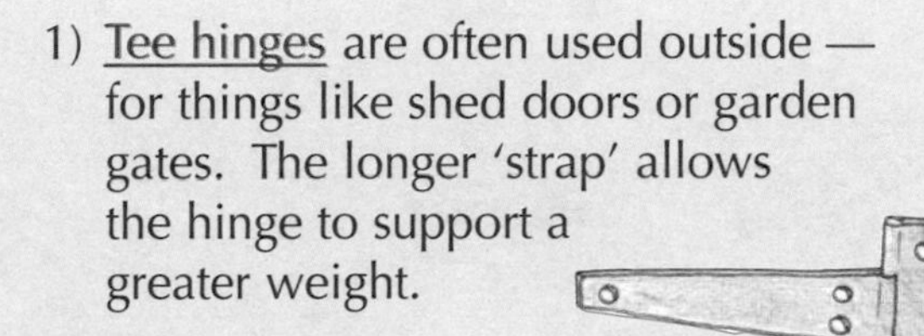

1) Pivot hinges are used when you might need to lift a door off its frame.
2) One part of the hinge is screwed to the door and the other to the door frame.

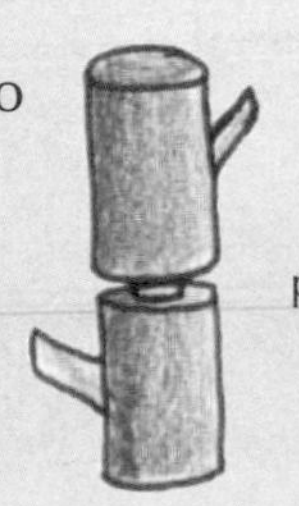

Two separate parts that fit together

Check around the house for examples of different hinges

A couple of these hinges have names that relate to their function and shape, which should help you to remember them. Others don't. A table showing sketches, functions and example uses could help.

Fixtures and Fittings

Most locks and catches are made from steel or brass

Locks need to be strong, and so tend to be made from steel, plated steel or brass.

Locks

1) Cupboard locks are screwed to the edge of cupboard doors.
2) No cutting is required when fitting the lock.
3) They can be used for both left and right locking.

Catches

1) Catches hold a door closed without locking.
2) They can be made out of brass, steel and various plastics.

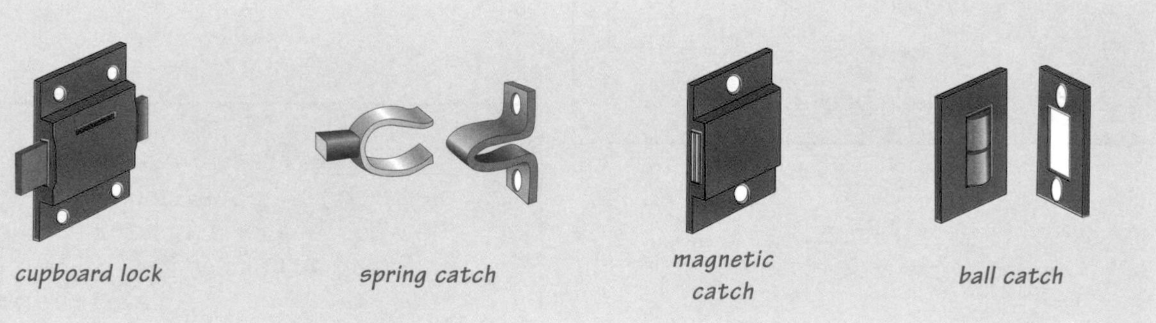

Other fixtures and fittings

1) Shelving fitments allow a shelf to be placed into position.
2) They do not require cutting into the shelf.
3) The fitments are able to be repositioned for different shelf heights.

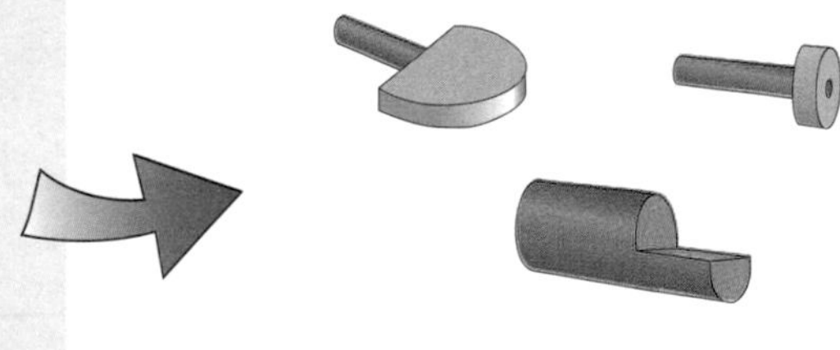

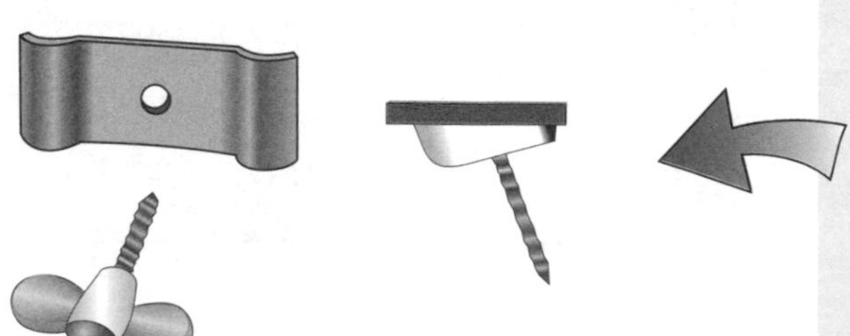

1) Leg fastenings can be used to attach legs to tables or chairs where the joints need to be frequently taken apart.
2) They also offer reinforcement, making the joint stronger.

There are a range of fixtures to suit different materials and situations

Each of these fittings and fixtures has its own advantages.
Learn the main features of each one... there's not too much detail here.

Adhesives

Adhesives are used for joining materials together.
The kind you need to use depends on what materials you're joining.

Polyvinyl acetate (PVA) is used for wood

1) Polyvinyl acetate (PVA) is a white woodworking glue.
2) There are two types of PVA — interior and exterior.
3) Interior will join wood as long as it doesn't get wet.
4) Exterior is more expensive, but is able to resist breaking down in damp conditions.
5) PVA is white and creamy and easy to use.

Contact adhesive is very strong

1) This glue is rubber based, and forms a very strong bond.
2) It's applied to both surfaces, and then the surfaces are kept apart for about 10 minutes until the glue goes tacky.
3) Then, when the surfaces are brought into contact, the sticking is instant.
4) Contact adhesive has a strong, unpleasant odour — so it's best used in a well-ventilated area.

Epoxy resin sticks almost anything

1) The trade name for epoxy resin is Araldite.
2) Two separate substances are mixed in equal parts — they're both thick, sticky liquids, but one is yellow and one is clear.
3) Once mixed, epoxy resin will stick almost anything — ceramic to ceramic, metal to wood, wood to plastic, etc.
4) It takes about 15 minutes to harden and is expensive.

Superglue also sticks most things

1) Superglue is even more expensive than epoxy resin but will stick to most things.
2) It certainly sticks to skin, so you have to be very careful.
3) It's a thin, clear liquid.
4) After applying the glue, slight pressure is required for a very strong bond.

Acrylic cement is used for plastics

1) Known as Tensol, this adhesive is used for plastics.
2) It's a watery, clear liquid.
3) Not particularly strong, but ideal for plastic objects where the joints aren't going to be knocked about.

Make a table of the different glues and their uses

There are a few things to remember on this page — names of the glues, their characteristics and the materials they're used to join. Write out those new terms until you're familiar with them.

Choosing the Best Material to Use

Selecting the right materials isn't easy. But it's something you've got to be able to do, otherwise you can end up wasting time and materials.

Different **factors** affect your **selection of material**

You should be able to make a good choice if you consider these factors:

Functional requirements — What does the material or product have to do?

Ask yourself the following questions:

1) What demands will be made on the material? (Will it have to withstand heavy loads or chemicals? Will it have to conduct heat or electricity?)
2) Will it be for outdoor or indoor use? (If it's for outside, you'll need to consider whether your material will corrode.)
3) Does it need to fit in with an environment? (Your material might need to be a particular style or have a certain look.)

Economics — How much money have you got?

You'll need to consider the following points:

1) The size of the product — materials like pewter are expensive, but may be a good choice for a small item of jewellery.
2) Scale of production — is your product a one-off, or will it be batch or mass produced? Stainless steel might be a good material for a one-off product. But if you're mass-producing something that would be equally as good made from some kind of plastic, that might be cheaper.

Availability of supply — What can you get hold of?

Can you get hold of the material you want? And if you can, can you get it in a suitable form? Most materials are only available in standard forms and sizes, and it can be very expensive to get a material in any other form. This will have a direct effect on the cost and the method of manufacture.

For example, materials might be available as granules, strips, bars, tubes, rough sawn, planed...

Manufacturing method — How will the product be made?

1) Some materials are easier to join than others (which will affect the production method used).
2) Also, the material must be suitable for the intended production method (and vice versa). For example, you can make something out of certain plastics using injection moulding, but it's no good planning to use this technique for wood.

So, take time and thought to weigh up the options ...

You need to know about different materials so you can choose the right one for the job in hand. It sounds obvious, but it's a mistake that amateurs make too often. Be smart — don't be one of them.

Warm-Up and Worked Exam Questions

Hinges, locks, catches and glue — it doesn't get any better than this. But have you been learning or just having fun... use these questions to find out.

Warm-up Questions

1) Sketch a flush hinge. What are they usually used for?
2) What materials are hinges commonly made out of?
3) What is a catch?
4) What does PVA stand for?
5) List these glues in order of expensiveness: epoxy resin, PVA, superglue.
6) What materials is acrylic cement used to join?
7) Give three functional requirements you might consider when choosing what material to use.

Worked Exam Question

These worked questions aren't here to aid your laziness. They're here to give you useful hints on decoding and answering exam questions. Don't rush them — use them wisely, my young apprentice.

1 Complete the table below by sketching and describing the hinges named. The first one has been done for you.

Make sure your sketches are nice and clear. But don't spend hours on each one — it's just a sketch.

	Butt hinge	Pivot hinge	Tee hinge
Sketch			
Description	Strong hinge, used for hanging doors	*Used for hanging doors, allows the door to be lifted off its frame.*	*Used outside, long strap allows it to support greater weight.*

(4 marks)

They mentioned two things in their butt hinge description — that's a clue to put two details in your descriptions.

Exam Questions

(a) A product is being constructed that is intended to be used out of doors. Two parts of the product are made of wood. Suggest a suitable glue to join these parts together.

....

(1 mark)

(b) A manufacturer is designing a new item of bedroom furniture. The product will require various glued joints of the plastic, wooden and metal parts.

(i) Name a suitable glue to use, if the manufacturer wishes to use the same glue to make all the joints.

....

(1 mark)

(ii) If cost is the main consideration, what would be a suitable glue to use for joints between two wooden components?

....

(1 mark)

(c) Name a suitable glue to join plastic components, where a strong bond is not required.

....

(1 mark)

3 A manufacturer is selecting what materials to use in a new product. They can choose from the materials described in the table on the right.

Material	Cost	Corrosion Resistance	Standard forms available	Finish comment
X	Cheap	Poor	Bars, rods, tubes	Attractive
Y	Expensive	Good	Sheets	Attractive
Z	Cheap	Poor	Bars, rods, sheets	Unattractive

(a) Which material would be suitable to use if the manufacturer's main consideration was how well the product would survive outside?

....

(1 mark)

(b) Compare the suitability of materials Z and Y for use in making handles for garden gates, as shown in this diagram.

....

....

....

....

(4 marks)

Revision Summary for Section Three

This section is packed fuller than a Des O'Connor concert with facts and properties about materials. It may not be particularly riveting, but it's definitely stuff you need to know. So try these questions, and if you get any wrong, go back, check the section and then try them again. And repeat this process until you get every single question right.

1) Name six mechanical properties, and describe what they mean.
2) Explain the difference between ferrous and non-ferrous metals. Give two examples of each.
3) What is an alloy?
4) What is meant by the following terms: a) annealing b) hardening c) tempering?
5) Suggest two surface finishes for metal.
6) Name the two different kinds of plastic. How are they different? Give two examples of each.
7) What is plastizote?
8) What are the two main categories of wood? Why are they different? Give two examples of each.
9) Describe three types of protective coating you could apply to wood.
10) Name one type of paint that is waterproof.
11) What is the main advantage of using plywood compared to solid wood?
12) Why are the layers in plywood glued at right angles to each other?
13) What is a 'veneer'? Why are veneers used?
14) Describe the main difference between blockboard and laminboard.
15) What does MDF stand for?
16) How is chipboard made?
17) What is a composite material?
18) Name two composite materials and explain why they are so useful.
19) Describe the special properties of a shape memory alloy.
20) What are the four main types of hinge? Describe when each type might be used.
21) Explain the difference between a lock and a catch.
22) Name five different types of adhesive. Explain when each type might be used, and what properties make it suitable for this use.
23) Name four factors that would affect your choice of material for a product you were going to make. Explain how each factor might influence your choice.

Systems

It's often handy to think of a device as a 'system'.
A system has various parts that work together to perform a set function.
In D&T, systems may include the use of mechanisms, electronics, pneumatics and structures.

Systems can be broken down into three simple elements:

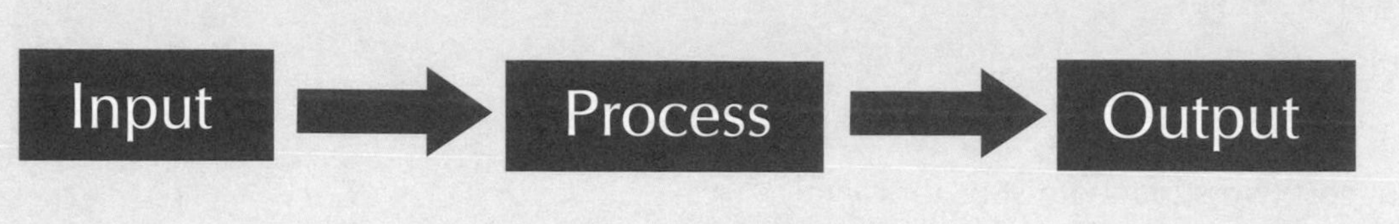

Subsystems — small components of a larger system

1) All complex systems can be broken down into a number of smaller systems, called subsystems.

2) A simple example of this is a bicycle. As a whole system it has:
   - an input — movement of your legs
   - a process — turning the pedals, which link to the wheels
   - an output — forward motion

You can break it down further into smaller subsystems like this:

Wheels and frame — a structural subsystem.
Pedals and gears — a mechanical subsystem.
Braking system — a mechanical or pneumatic subsystem.

Try applying your knowledge to other systems...

Breaking down systems into their basic parts is crucial. Applying your knowledge of subsystems and inputs, outputs and processes can make even very complicated systems seem manageable.

Mechanical Systems and Movement

Pay attention — this stuff on mechanical advantage isn't hard, but it's essential to the topic. And you're bound to get a question on those four types of motion in the exam.

Mechanical systems — systems that use mechanisms

1) In Resistant Materials you need to look in detail at mechanical systems.
2) All mechanical systems will have mechanisms that transform an input motion and force into a desired output motion and force.
3) They will be designed so that you can gain some advantage from using them — in other words they make something easier for you to do. This idea is known as '*mechanical advantage*'.
4) For example, a car jack lets you lift up a car, a job you couldn't do without it. The mechanism gives you an advantage.

Motion — the different way things move

In this section you will be looking at a number of different mechanisms, many of which are designed to change one type of motion into another. You need to understand four different types of motion:

1) Linear Motion — moving in a straight line.

Linear

2) Rotary Motion — moving in a circle, e.g. a wheel.

Rotary

3) Oscillating Motion — moving backwards and forwards in an arc, e.g. a swing.

Oscillating

4) Reciprocating Motion — moving backwards and forwards in a straight line.

Reciprocating

Systems, subsystems and four types of motion

These two topics — systems and motion — are important to learn at this stage. They're the basics. So you need to know them well before you move on.

Gear Mechanisms

The 'process' part of a system could include one or more mechanisms. The next few pages are about making sure you know about all the main kinds of mechanism. First — gears.
Gears are toothed wheels which interlock (or mesh) together as a way of transmitting rotary motion.

Gear train — linking gears together

Where two or more gears are linked together it is called a gear train.

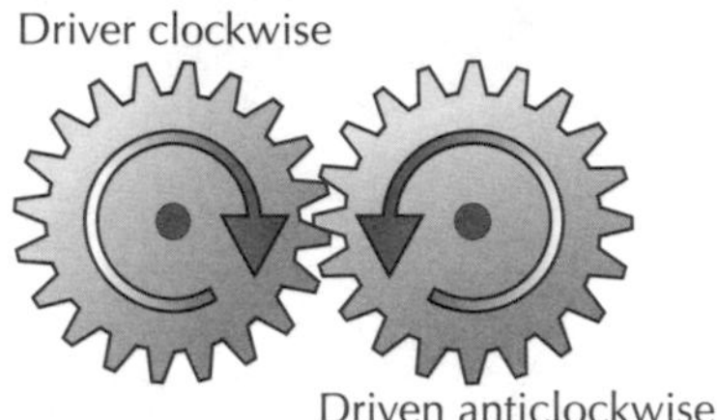

The DRIVER GEAR, turned by hand or motor (the input), turns the driven gear (the output). Both will automatically turn in different directions. If the driver is turning clockwise, the driven will turn anticlockwise and vice versa.

By using a third gear called an IDLER, the driver and the driven gears will both turn in the same direction. The size of the idler will not alter the speed of the other two gears.

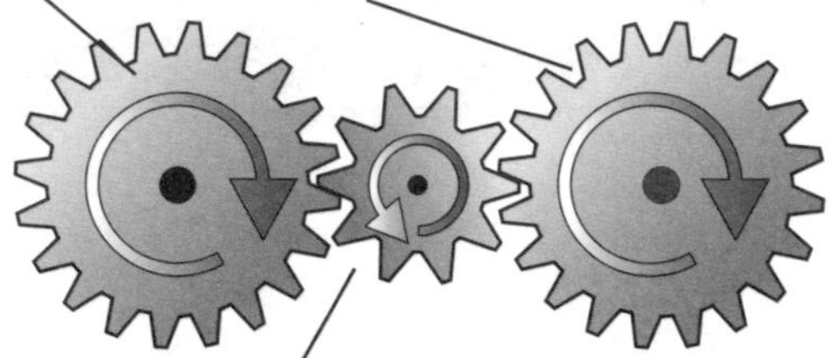

If linked gears are different sizes, they will turn at different speeds. The GEAR RATIO is the relationship between the number of teeth on the driver gear and the driven gear. Any idler gears will have no effect on the gear ratio.

A COMPOUND gear train is where more than one gear is fixed to the same shaft. This is handy because it lets you change the gear ratio easily.

Gears — toothed wheels that interlock to transmit rotary motion

It's worth making sure you're familiar with each of the terms here — driver gear, driven gear, idler, gear ratio and compound gear trains. You'll need to use all of this stuff in the next few pages.

Gear Mechanisms

The gears on this page are a bit more complex. These gears don't just change the direction and speed of motion, they can also change the type of motion too, e.g. from rotary into linear.

Gears can change the **type** and **direction** of motion

1. RACK AND PINION gears are used to turn rotary motion into linear motion. The pinion, a round gear, is turned to move a flat gear, the rack.

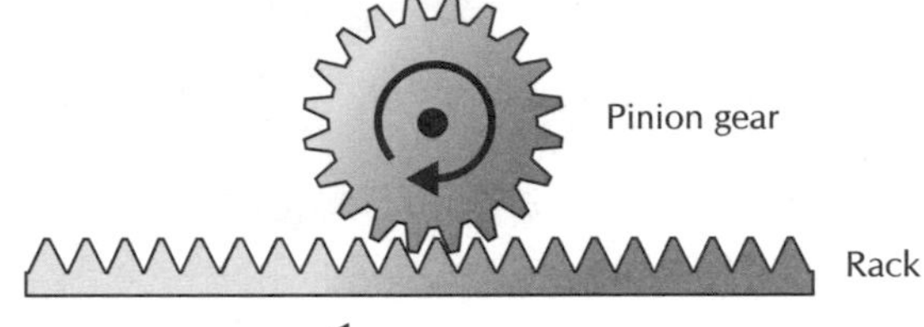

2. A WORM DRIVE AND WORM WHEEL change the direction of rotation through 90°. The worm drive (the driver) only has one tooth and will turn much faster than the worm wheel, which with many teeth will turn very slowly.

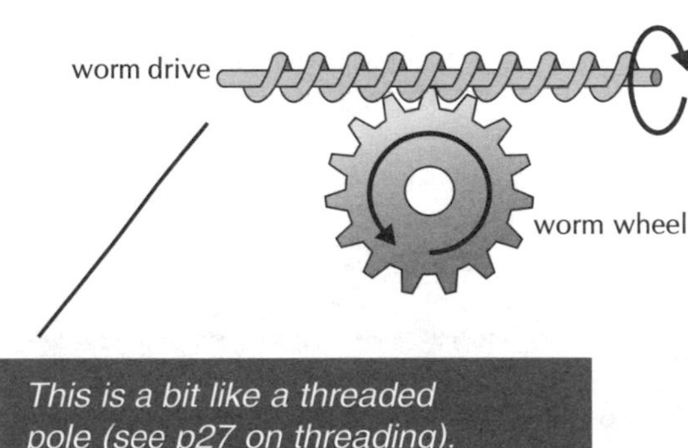

This is a bit like a threaded pole (see p27 on threading). This thread acts as one big 'tooth'.

3. BEVEL GEARS also change the direction of rotation through 90°.

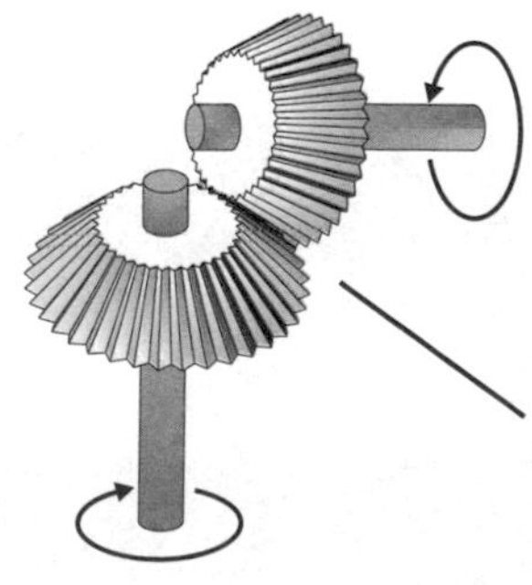

The teeth are angled at 45° so the gears fit together at right angles.

You need to be able to sketch and label these gear mechanisms

You also need to be able to describe what's happening. Remember — gear trains can change the direction and speed of rotary motion. Rack and pinion can also change the type of motion.

Belt Drives, Chains and Velocity Ratio

Read this page carefully, and make sure you've got it learnt.
You need to be able to use those formulas for the exam.

Belt drives transfer power and movement

1) A belt drive transfers power and movement from one rotating shaft to another.
2) Belt drives are used in pillar drills. The flexible belt links the motor to the drill shaft, and can be put in different positions to make the drill turn faster or slower.

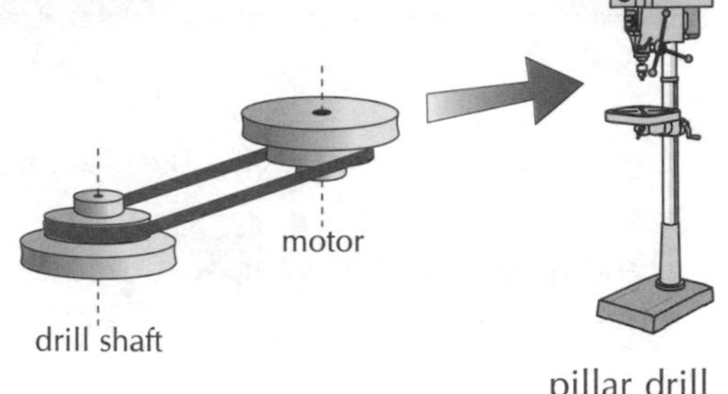

pillar drill

Chain and sprockets transfer power and movement

1) A common example of a chain and sprocket mechanism is on a bike.
2) There are two sprockets (toothed wheels) linked with a chain (made up from loads of links).
3) This has the advantage that it doesn't slip like a belt drive can.

chain sprocket

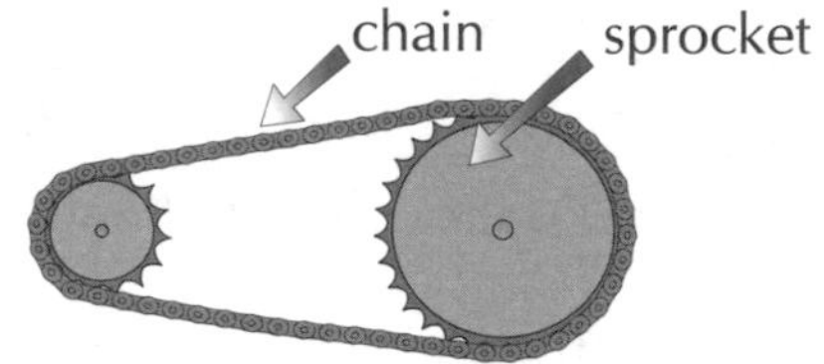

Velocity ratio — to work out speeds

1) With both of the above systems, if you alter the size of the wheels or sprockets, you change the speed that they turn.
2) The relationship between the two is summed up by the velocity ratio.
3) With both systems, simple formulas will help you calculate the velocities:

RPM — Revolutions Per Minute

Belt Drives

$$\text{RPM of the driven pulley} = \frac{\text{RPM of driver pulley} \times \text{diameter of driver pulley}}{\text{diameter of driven pulley}}$$

Chain and Sprockets

$$\text{Velocity ratio} = \frac{\text{Number of teeth on the driven sprocket}}{\text{Number of teeth on the driver sprocket}}$$

You need to know these formulas for the exam...

Make sure you learn those formulas. Make up a few simple examples (and sketch them) and try out the formulas on them — they make a lot more sense when you try them with actual numbers.

Warm-Up and Worked Exam Questions

There's no point in skimming through the section and glancing over the questions — you won't learn anything, you fools. Do the warm-up questions and go back over any bits you don't know. Then practise and practise the exam questions.

Warm-up Questions

1) What three elements make up a system?
2) What's the difference between oscillating motion, and reciprocating motion?
3) What is an idler gear?
4) Sketch and label a rack and pinion gear.
5) How does a belt drive work?
6) In the context of a chain and sprocket, what is the "velocity ratio"?

Worked Exam Question

Wow, an exam question — with the answers helpfully written in. It must be your lucky day.

1 The diagram below shows a simple gear train.

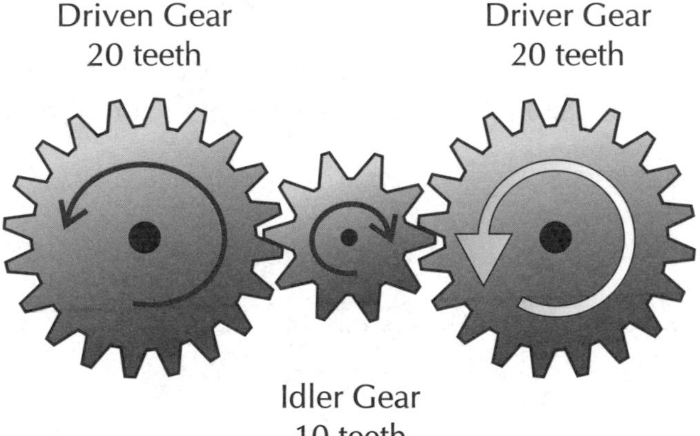

The driver gear is going anti-clockwise and you can see how it will push the idler gear clockwise... which will push the driven gear anti-clockwise... (Each gear goes the opposite way to the one(s) it's connected to.)

(a) Draw arrows on the diagram to show the direction of motion of the idler and driven gears.

(2 marks)

(b) How will the speed of motion of the driven gear and the driver gear compare?

They will be the same.

(1 mark)

Count the teeth — the driver and driven gears both have the same number. (Remember — the idler doesn't make a difference.)

Exam Questions

2 The diagram below shows a music box.
As the handle is turned clockwise, the music cylinder turns clockwise.

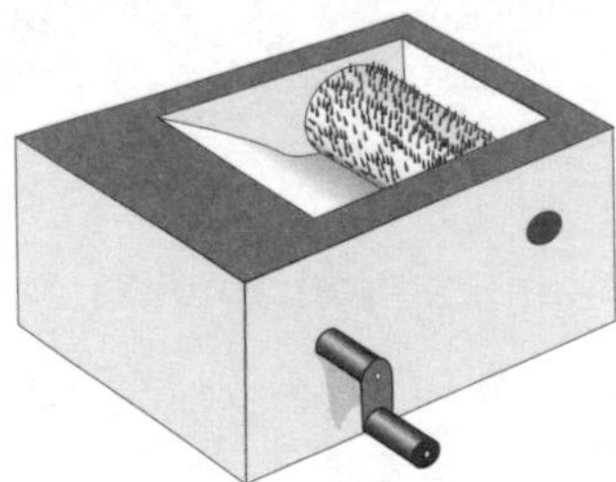

(a) The diagram below shows how the handle shaft and music cylinder shaft could be connected by a belt drive.

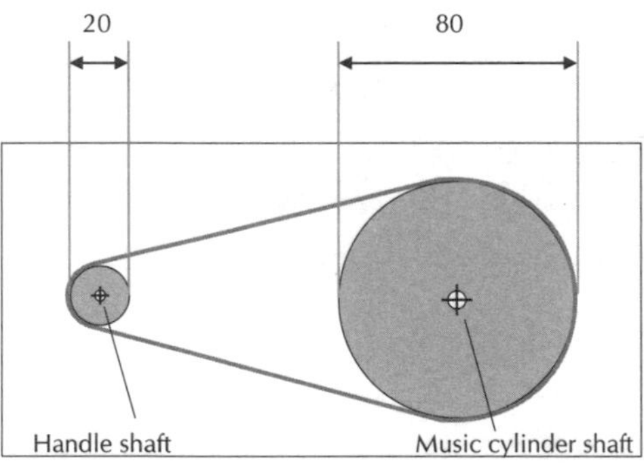

In the arrangement shown, if the handle shaft rotates once every second, how quickly will the music cylinder shaft rotate? Show your workings.

....

....

....

(2 marks)

(b) A chain and sprockets could be used instead of a belt drive.
On the diagram below, draw and label a suitable chain and sprocket mechanism that would make the music cylinder rotate twice for every rotation of the handle shaft.

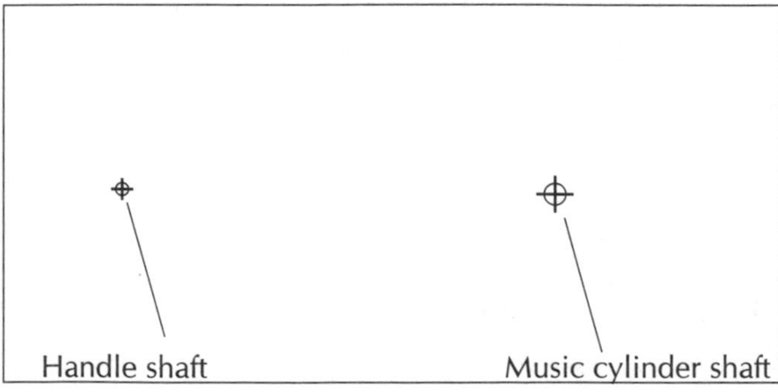

(4 marks)

Pulleys and Cams

Pulleys can help you gain mechanical advantage when lifting

1) Pulleys are a way of gaining mechanical advantage when lifting a load.

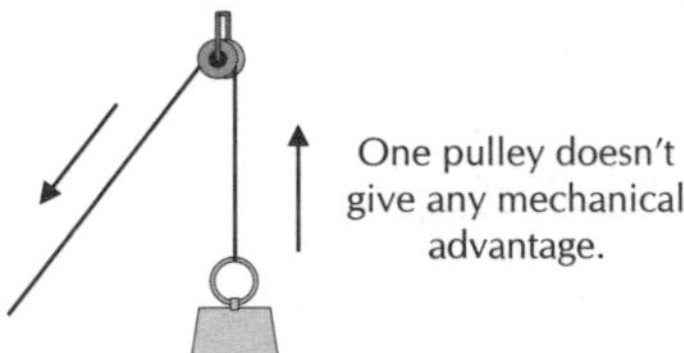

2) One pulley on its own will not make a load lighter, but it will reverse the direction of the force required. You will be able to lift the load by pulling.

3) If set up in the correct way pulleys can make things appear a lot lighter than they actually are. For example, one fixed pulley and one moving pulley (a block and tackle) will mean you only need half the force.

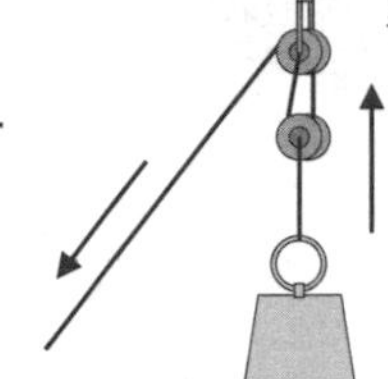

Simple Block and Tackle

Weight can be lifted using half the effort.

You don't need to know why this works — but if you really want to find out, try starting with an A-Level mechanics book...

Cams — change rotary motion into reciprocating motion

1) A cam is a mechanism that converts rotary motion into reciprocating motion.
2) The cam mechanism has two main parts — the cam itself and the follower.
3) The cam is a rotating shape that comes in many different shapes and sizes.
4) The follower follows the shape of the cam. It may simply rest on the cam, or it may have a small wheel to reduce friction.

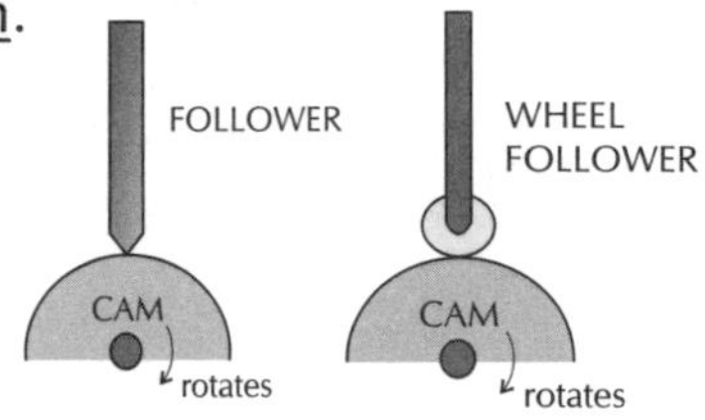

Here are a few basic cam shapes that you need to be able to recognise:

1) CIRCULAR CAM — Also called offset or eccentric — produces a uniform reciprocating motion.

The circular cam rotates about an off-centre pivot...

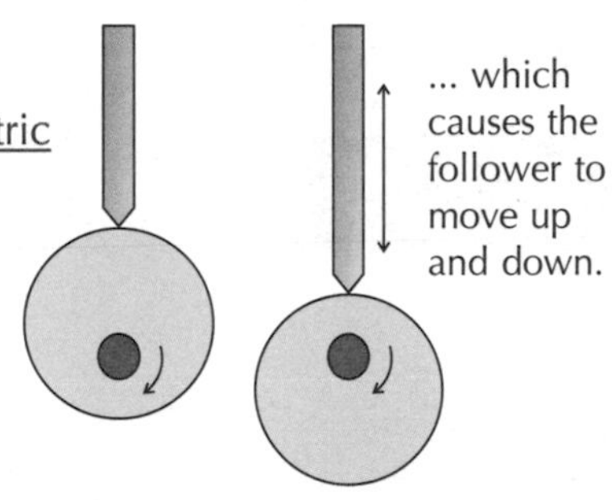

... which causes the follower to move up and down.

2) SNAIL CAM — For half of the revolution the follower will not move, then it will gently rise, and then suddenly drop. It will only work in one direction.

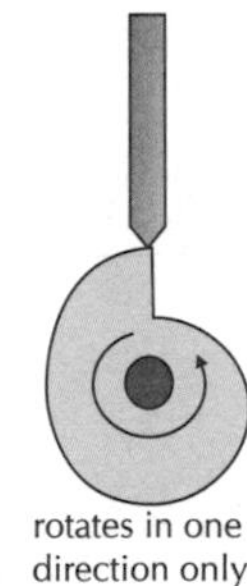

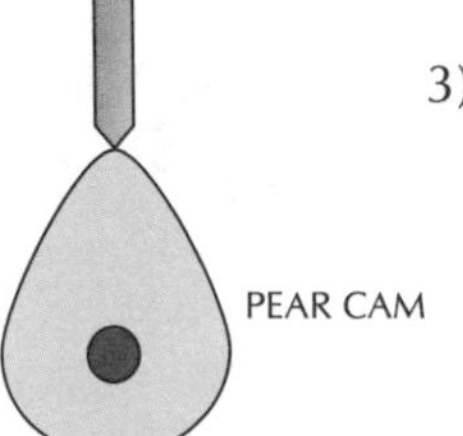

3) PEAR CAM — Again for half a revolution the follower will not move, then it will gently rise and fall.

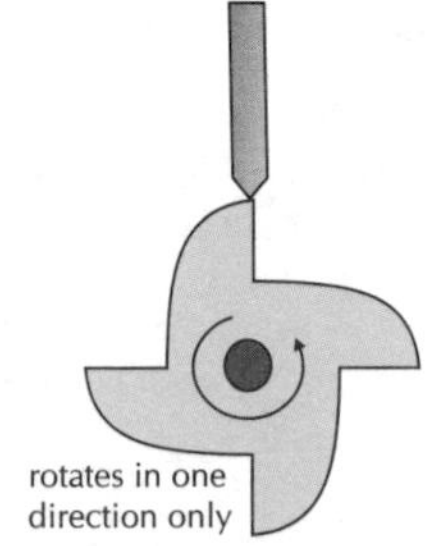

4) FOUR-LOBED CAM — Has four lobes (bits that stick out). For each turn of the cam the follower will rise and suddenly fall four times. This cam shape will also only work in one direction.

Pulleys make life easier, cams make life a bit different...

Always keep the movement of the follower in mind when you're working on cams. Try to imagine the reciprocating motion that each of these cams create. The whole thing's easier to learn if you can picture it.

Cranks

Cranks are used all over the place — from simple mechanical toys to car engines, valves and pumps.

Cranks — the simplest crank is a **handle** on a **shaft**

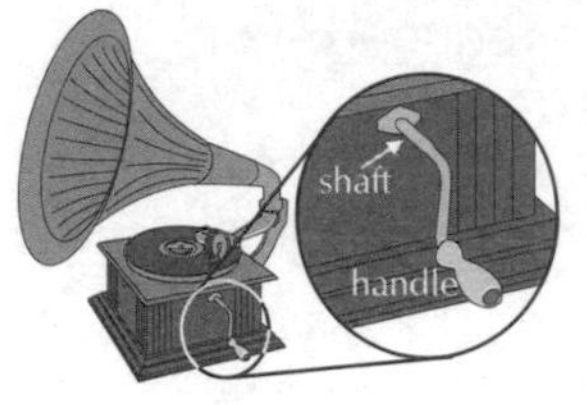

1) A crank can be as simple as a handle on a shaft. As you increase the distance between the handle and the shaft, the handle gets easier to turn (you have a greater mechanical advantage).

2) Cranks can be used with connecting rods to turn rotation into reciprocating motion (up and down), like in a toy car where the driver's head bobs up and down.

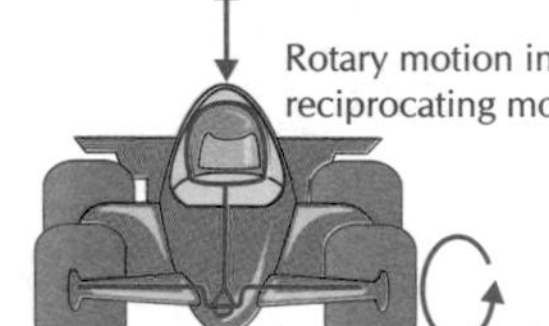

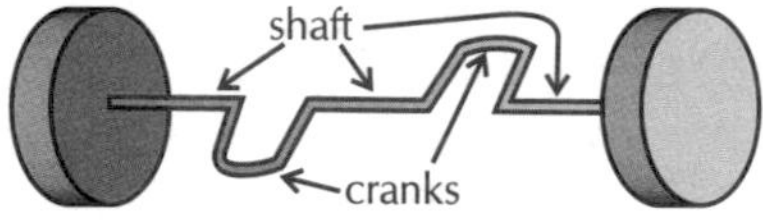

3) When a crank or several cranks are directly on the shaft it is called a crankshaft. They're used on kids' go-carts as a simple pedalling mechanism.

Crank and slider — as seen in **pistons**

1) This mechanism can be found in steam engines. The reciprocating motion of a piston is turned into rotational motion.

2) Both parts are joined together with a connecting rod. The mechanism won't work unless the rod can move at both ends.

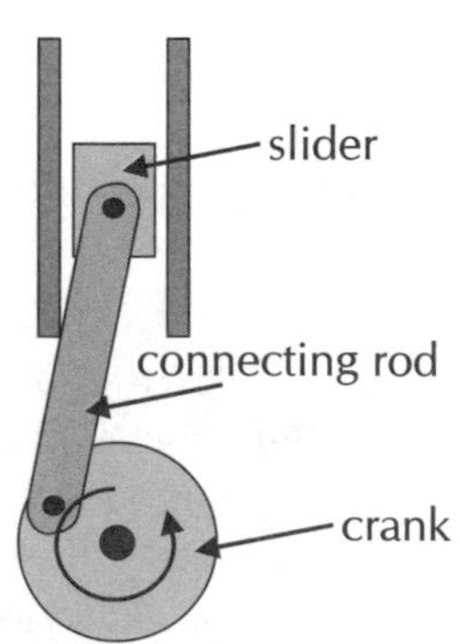

Cranks are another method of gaining mechanical advantage

Cams turn rotation into reciprocating motion.
Cranks can do the same and they can also do the opposite.

Levers

Levers are used to help move or lift things.
There are three different types of lever that you will need to know about.

First class lever — pivot in the middle

1) All first class levers have the pivot between the effort and the load.
2) By using this type of lever a large load can be lifted using a smaller effort — the lever gives you a mechanical advantage.
3) As you move the pivot closer to the load it becomes easier to lift.

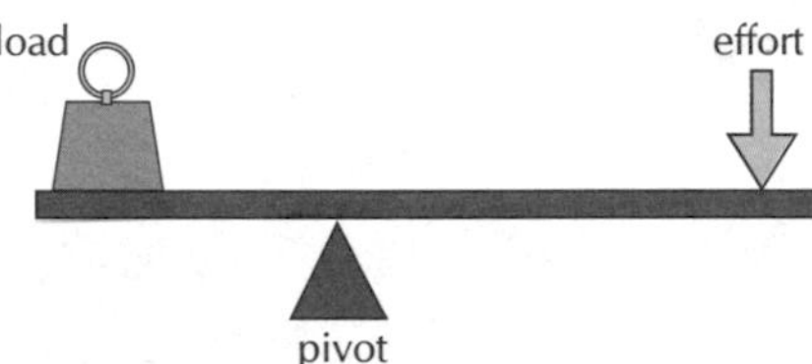

Second class lever — load in the middle

1) Here the pivot is at one end of the lever and the effort is at the other end.
2) Again the closer you put the pivot and the load, the easier it is to lift.

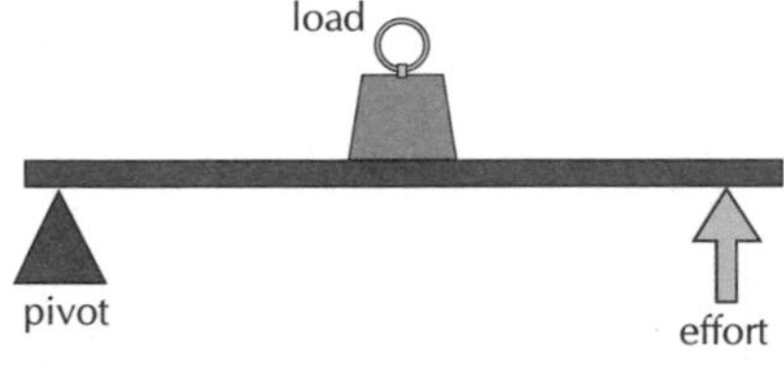

A wheelbarrow is a good example of a second class lever

Third class lever — effort in the middle

1) In a third class lever the effort is in between the load and the pivot.
2) Third class levers can be things like fishing rods, cricket bats and garden spades.
3) Moving the effort and pivot apart makes it easier to move/lift the load.

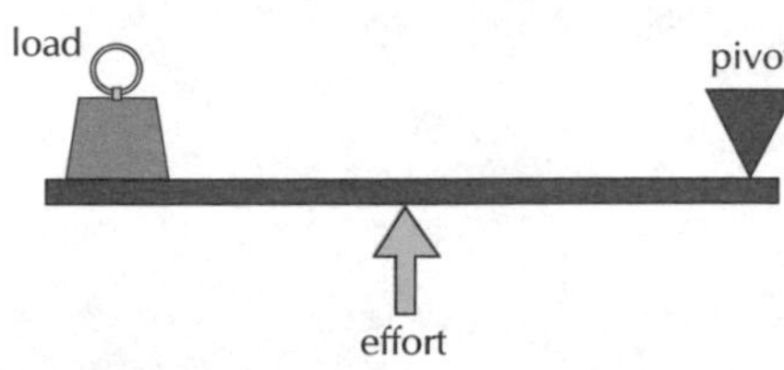

Load, effort, pivot — learn the classes of lever and examples

As usual, the best way to learn is to sketch and describe what you remember until you know it all. Now you are beginning to understand that Resistant Materials is truly a subject of art and creativity.

Double-Acting Levers and Links

This page looks a bit more complicated — but it's basically about building on stuff you've already covered.

Double-acting levers — first class levers joined together

Sometimes levers can be joined together. A double-acting lever is when you have two first class levers hinged together at the pivot point. A common example of this is a pair of scissors.

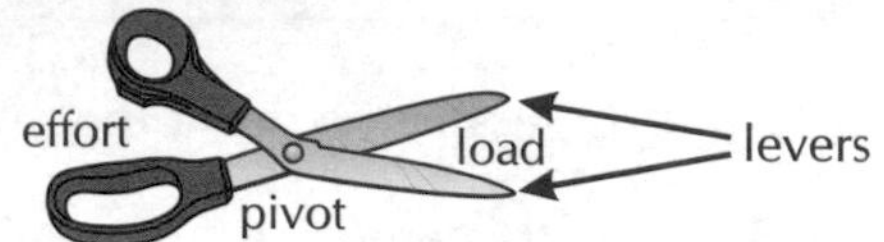

Links connect different parts of a mechanism

A link is something that connects different parts of a mechanism together. Here are a few common examples:

1) Simple links can:
   - transfer forces and
   - change the direction of motion.

2) A bell crank changes the direction of a force through 90°.

3) Lazy tongs use loads of levers linked together.

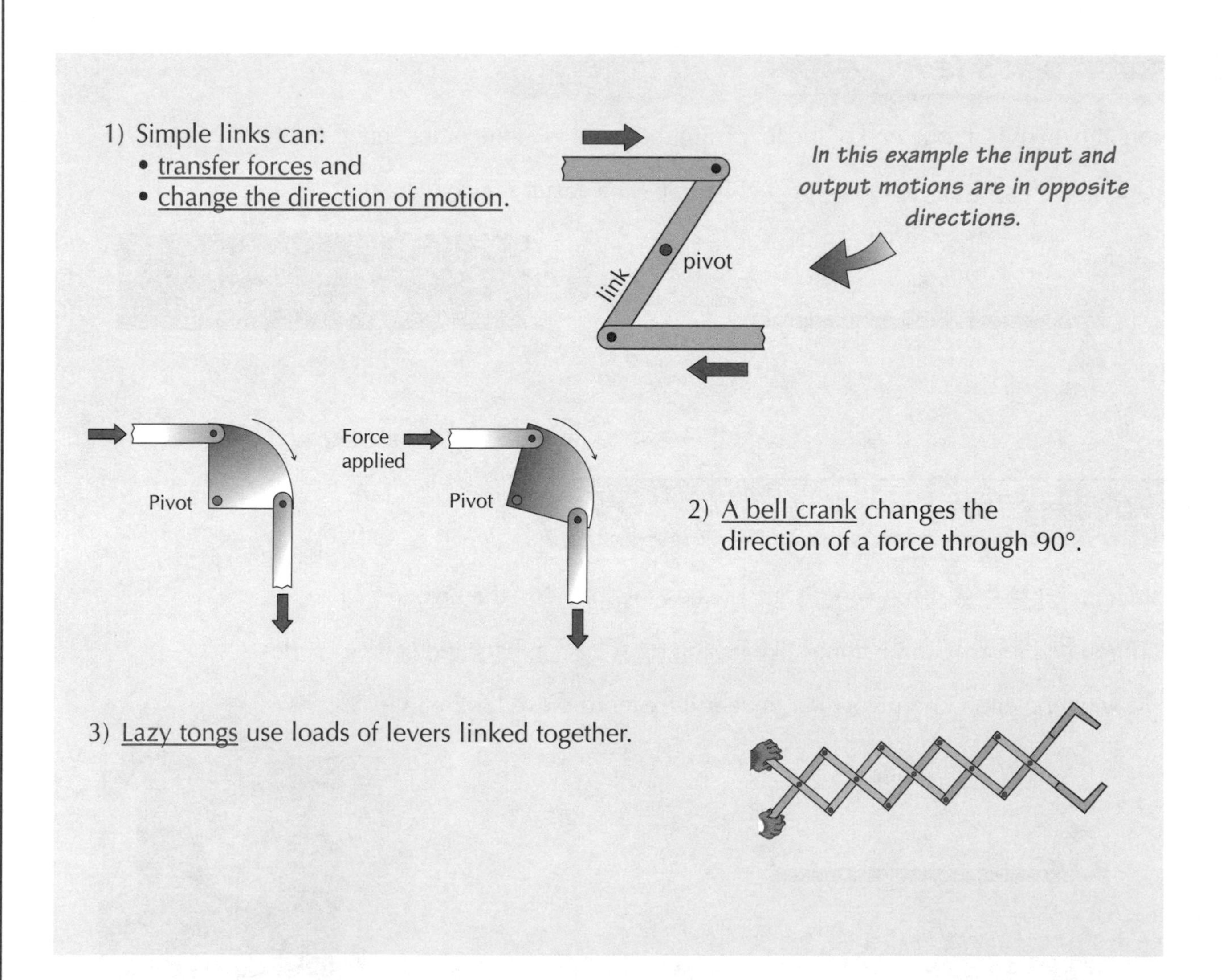

More about mechanical advantage and changing motion...

This stuff isn't that bad. Double-acting levers and links are just an extension of what you've learned already. Don't let it stress you out. If you don't get it, go back and look at page 75 again.

Warm-Up and Worked Exam Questions

Warm up questions first, then a worked example, then you're on your own. You know the routine...

Warm-up Questions

1) Sketch a block and tackle being used to lift a weight.
2) What is a cam?
3) Describe the movement of the follower on a snail cam.
4) "Cranks can be used to turn rotation into reciprocating motion." What does that mean in plain English?
5) What's the difference between first, second and third class levers?
6) What does a bell crank do?

Worked Exam Question

Don't rush this worked example because... it's got a banana in it.

1 A greengrocer has bought a moving banana device for her shop window, as shown in the diagram below.

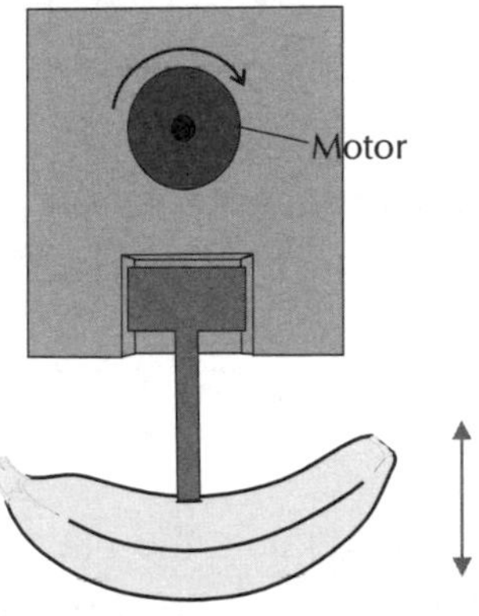

(a) What type of motion is made by the banana?

Reciprocating motion.

NB — Only the proper term will do. "Uppy and downy" won't get the marks.

(1 mark)

(b) The device requires a linkage mechanism in order to make the banana move as desired. Complete the diagram below to show this linkage mechanism. Label your diagram.

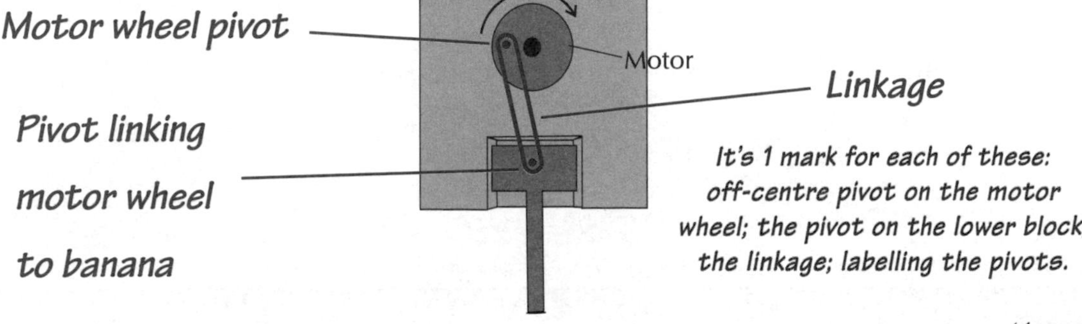

(4 marks)

Exam Questions

2 A moving Christmas decoration has been made, as shown in the diagram below.

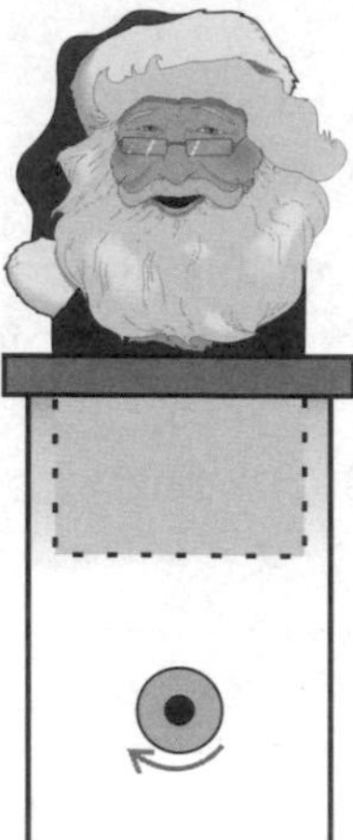

(a) As the motor turns, the Father Christmas slowly rises and falls, and then remains still for a short while. Draw a mechanism on the diagram above that would cause the Father Christmas to move in this way.

(2 marks)

(b) Give the name of the mechanism you have drawn.

....

(1 mark)

(c) Draw a mechanism that would make the Father Christmas continually slowly rise and fall with no still period.

(1 mark)

(d) Give the name of the mechanism you have drawn.

....

(1 mark)

Revision Summary for Section Four

Mechanisms probably isn't *the most* fascinating topic you've ever read about. But it's pretty easy, really, so there's no excuse for not learning all the examples in this section. There's nearly always a question on mechanisms in the exam — you might have to incorporate a particular mechanism into a design and for this you need to know a range of examples, what they do and how they do it.
The questions below test what you've learned — get on with them.

1) Describe the three elements that any system can be broken down into.
2) Some large systems can be split into smaller systems.
What are the smaller systems called?
3) Describe three subsystems of a bicycle.
4) What is mechanical advantage?
5) List and describe, with the aid of simple diagrams, four different types of motion.
6) Give a simple explanation of what gears do.
7) What is a gear train?
8) What is the difference between a driven gear and a driver gear?
9) Describe the purpose of an idler gear.
10) Will altering the size of the idler gear change the speed of the driver and driven gear?
11) Explain the term 'gear ratio' and give an example of how it is calculated.
12) What's the advantage of using a compound gear train?
13) Sketch a rack and pinion gear mechanism. Describe the motion involved.
14) Which turns faster — a worm drive or a worm wheel? Explain your answer.
15) What does a bevel gear do?
16) Explain what a belt drive is and give a simple example.
17) What is the advantage of using a chain and sprocket mechanism instead of a belt drive?
18) What does 'velocity ratio' mean?
19) How can a pulley system give you mechanical advantage? Draw an example.
20) What are the two main parts of a cam mechanism?
21) Sketch and describe four different cam shapes.
22) Name two cam shapes can only rotate in one direction.
23) Give an example of where you might find a crank.
24) Where might you find a crank and slider mechanism?
25) Sketch and describe a first class lever, and give an example.
26) Sketch and describe a second class lever, and give an example.
27) Sketch and describe a third class lever, and give an example.
28) What is a double-acting lever?
29) Write a simple definition of a link.
30) What two things can a link do?
31) Sketch a bell crank and describe what it does.
32) Sketch a pair of lazy tongs.

Product Analysis

You've no hope of designing good products if you don't look at what other people have done first — all designers do it. You need to work out what makes them work and what makes the designs good.

Analysing *existing products makes you a* ***better designer***

Product analysis is essential (for all designers) because it helps you:

1) think about what makes a good design
2) think about manufacturing methods
3) understand the uses of different materials
4) get ideas to use in your own designs, or modify existing designs based on what you find out
5) pick out examples of good or bad design, manufacture and material selection
6) make better judgements about what products people might buy

Consider all these ***factors*** *when* ***analysing*** *a product*

1. FUNCTION: Function is what the product is intended to be used for — and how it works. When analysing a product think about: what it's used for, whether it does its job well and whether it satisfies a need. *(See also page 2.)*

2. FORM: In other words, the shape and look of a product — e.g. colour, texture and decoration. A product could be old-fashioned or modern-looking. It could have flowing curves or it might be very angled with lots of corners. This is also known as 'aesthetics'. *(See also page 4.)*

3. ERGONOMICS: Ergonomics is about how easy the product is to use — whether it's safe and comfortable. A hand-held product needs to fit well in the hand, for example. Controls and buttons need to be easily reachable. Designers have to take all of these things into account. *(See also page 87.)*

Research and analysis are essential when designing a new product

Thinking about existing products is a brilliant way of getting some inspiration for your own designs. It's also a good way of learning to think critically about products that are already on the market.

Product Analysis

There are lots of points to remember here — make sure you can remember all the headings first, then try and tackle the detail.

There are lots of other factors to consider when analysing a product

4. COST: You need to consider value for money. If you were investigating a hairdryer, say, you could conduct a survey and find out if it's cheaper or more expensive than similar hairdryers.

5. COMPETITION: How it performs compared to other similar products on the market.

6. ENVIRONMENT: Some parts or components might be recyclable when the product reaches the end of its life. Some parts might be made from biodegradable materials. Manufacture is important, too — it might involve environmentally unfriendly processes. *(See also pages 86, 90-91.)*

7. MATERIALS: Product analysis should include looking at what materials have been used, why those materials were chosen and how those materials were formed or shaped.

8. MANUFACTURE: Consider all the processes that have been used to manufacture the product. This includes things like which technique was used to mould any plastic in the product, and how electrical parts have been used. Don't forget to check if any parts have been assembled separately and plonked into the product later — the term for that is sub-assembly.

9. DEVELOPMENT: Development is stuff that the manufacturer could do to improve the product. Development includes things they could do to make it more popular and increase sales.

Uncover the hidden mysteries of the product design world

Basically, you want to make sure that you've covered as much ground as possible when you're analysing a product. And, fortunately, it's all been reduced into nine simple points for you.

Quality Assurance and Quality Control

Quality Assurance (QA) is all about standards — setting standards and meeting them.
Quality Control (QC) is how you check that you're meeting those standards.

*Products are **monitored** for **quality***

- Products are monitored for quality right through from design and development to manufacture, end-use performance and degree of customer satisfaction.
- Top companies that do QA well are awarded ISO 9000 — an international standard of quality.
- Factors such as equipment, materials and staff training are constantly checked.

Quality Control** is **making sure** you're within **tolerances

Quality control involves testing a sample of a component at every stage of production. It stresses the importance of working to specific tolerances — i.e. margins of error.

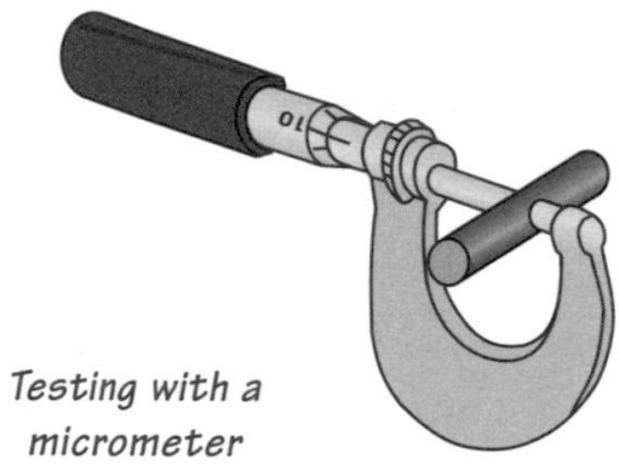

Testing with a micrometer

Tolerance in testing is expressed as an upper (+) and lower (–) deviation. For example, if a spindle is specified as being 20 mm (± 0.5), then a micrometer reading of between 19.5 mm and 20.5 mm would be OK.

Quality Control makes sure a product does these things:

1) conforms to the design specification
2) does the job it was designed to do
3) meets relevant standards institutions' criteria (pages 88-89)
4) keeps the customer happy

Quality Assurance = standards, Quality Control = checks

Know the difference. The last four points in the blue box describe why QC and QA are very important. You'll need to be able to discuss these for the exam.

Testing and TQM

*There are **different kinds** of testing*

Testing can identify faults with machining and tool settings and eliminate costly waste.

1) Measuring every component with a micrometer is a time-consuming (and therefore costly) business — this process can be speeded up using limit gauges. These are usually double-ended, one end being machined to the lower limit and the other end to the upper limit.

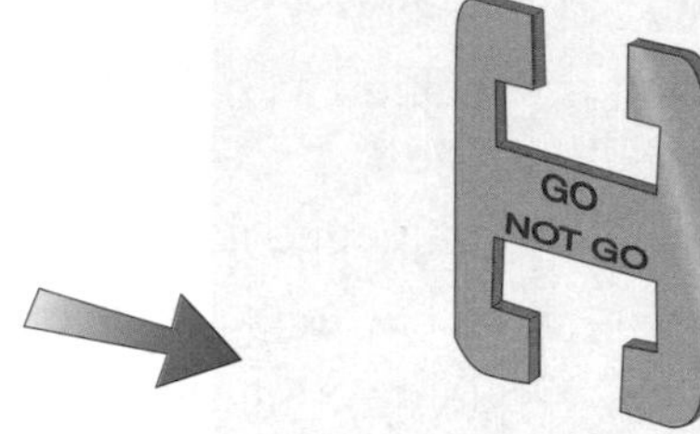

If the component fits through the upper limit but not the lower one, it's within the acceptable range.

2) Some testing is visual and may include using X-rays to spot defects, e.g. of a welded joint. This is called non-destructive testing.

3) Some testing is physical and destroys the product to see how fractures develop or to examine the nature of collapse. This is called destructive testing.

In your own project, your work needs testing and checking. You might need to make your own gauges and measuring tools, as well as using the trusty micrometer

***Total quality management** — LOTS of quality control*

'Total Quality Management' (TQM) introduces Quality Control systems at every stage of manufacture and management. TQM aims for right first time, every time.

TQM aims to ensure there are as few mistakes as possible

The important thing here is that you know how to do quality checks, and how to make sure that your components are the right size and shape and that they match your manufacturer's specification.

Warm-Up and Worked Exam Questions

This is quite an interesting section after all that stuff about tools, materials and gears. It's basically about looking at the final product you've got and deciding if it's up to scratch. Anyway, on with the questions...

Warm-up Questions

1) List the nine factors you should consider when developing a product.
2) What is ISO 9000 awarded for?
3) A component is specified as being 15 mm (± 0.4 mm) long, and it's measured with a micrometer and found to be 14.3 mm long. Is that OK?
4) Describe what a limit gauge is.
5) Is X-ray testing of welds an example of destructive or non-destructive testing?
6) In the context of quality control, what does TQM stand for?

Worked Exam Question

Trainspotters amongst you may recognise this particular train from page 9. (It is a fine model.)

1 The diagram below shows a toy train, designed for children aged 2-5 years.

Main Features

Yellow painted finish.

Windows and doors painted on.

Moveable wheels

The manufacturer wants to carry out quality control checks during the production of the toy.

(a) What is meant by Quality Control?

The testing of a product to make sure it meets the design specification and the standards set by the relevant standards' institutions.

(2 marks)

(b) Give **two** Quality Control checks that could be performed on the above product.

1 *Check dimensions of the components match the original specification.*

2 *Check the quality of the material.*

The quality of the joints, the operation of the wheels and the quality of the surface finish are other possible answers.

(2 marks)

Exam Questions

2 A manufacturer is producing batches of large metal pipes.
Each pipe must be 30 mm (± 0.2) in diameter.

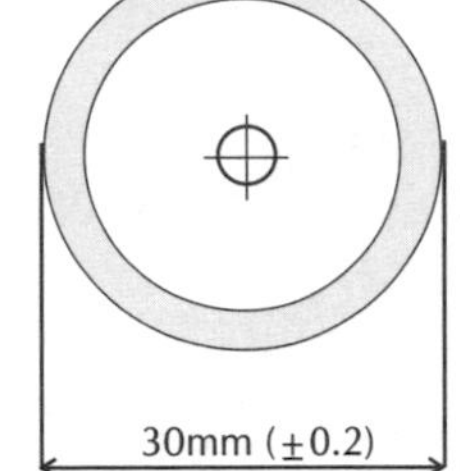

With notes and sketches, describe one method of quality control that you could use to ensure that the diameter of each pipe is acceptable.

(3 marks)

3 When designing a new product, designers often analyse existing products.
Suggest **three** ways in which such analysis can be useful for the designer.

1 ....

....
(1 mark)

2 ....

....
(1 mark)

3 ....

....
(1 mark)

Environmental and Social Responsibility

Social responsibility in design is all about making sure you don't make products that mess up people's health, people's lives or the environment.

Design must be **socially** and **environmentally responsible**

When you're selecting materials, components, and manufacturing processes, you need to take these factors into consideration:

1) whether using the product might harm people or the environment.
2) whether any materials used, including paints and varnishes, are toxic.
3) whether the manufacture of the product harms the environment, e.g. consider how much waste material will be produced by the manufacturing process, and how it's going to be disposed of.
4) whether recycled materials could be used to make the product or packaging — or biodegradable or recyclable materials, if the product's designed to be thrown away after use.
5) whether conditions for workers during manufacture will be of a good standard e.g. making sure manufacturing processes aren't hazardous.
6) whether any social, cultural or religious groups may be offended by the product.

Products must be **safe** and **easy to use**

When you're designing, think about how people are going to use the product.

1) The product must be safe to use, e.g. no sharp edges on toys. It's not socially responsible to injure your customers.
2) The product must be user-friendly. Take responsibility for the experience of using it. If the product is frustrating and difficult to use, it isn't well designed.
3) Think about whether the product could be misused. If people use a product for something that it hasn't been designed for, it might be dangerous.

Designers HAVE to think about these things

The point of thinking about social responsibility is to make sure people or the environment aren't harmed by your product. Pretty important. Being sued wouldn't do a company many favours.

Environmental and Social Responsibility

These are some of the issues designers and manufacturers need to think about when they're creating a new product. Make sure you can use examples when you're talking about ergonomics and social issues.

Ergonomics means making the product fit the user

1) Products need to be designed so that their size and proportions make them fit the needs of the user — e.g. a chair for a five-year-old needs to be a different size from a chair for a fifteen-year-old (obviously).

2) Designers use body measurement data, known as anthropometrics, to make sure that the product is the right size and shape for people to use.

3) For example, a chair seat needs to be the right height off the ground so that the person sitting in it has their feet on the floor, and their knees at a right angle. The back of the chair should support the person's back in the right place.

4) Badly designed products can have long-term health impacts. They might well be safe to use on a day-to-day basis (e.g. there's no risk of losing a limb), but end up causing things like eye strain or backache after long-term use.

*There are **social issues** concerned with products aimed at **kids***

1) Parents often have strong views on what sort of products they want their kids to use.

2) Society often has something to say, too — e.g. a hand-held games console might be criticised because it encourages kids to sit around all day, hunched over a tiny screen instead of running about and getting fresh air.

Ergonomics — it's about comfort and health

Social responsibility is about making sure the manufacture & use of products doesn't harm any people or the environment. Scribble a paragraph to say why these issues are important when designing a product.

Consumers

What the customer wants or needs drives all design briefs. Without customers, there's no need for the product. If no one buys a manufacturer's products, the manufacturer will go bust.

Customer satisfaction *is what manufacturers want*

If you just think about design as what you do in D&T lessons, you might see evaluation as the end of the design process. In the world of manufacturing,the end of the process is customer satisfaction...

- Customer satisfaction is achieved when the product works, is great to use, and is good value for money.
- For this to happen, product development, design, production, engineering, marketing and finance all need to work properly together and become a quality system.
- The key features of a quality system are quality control (QC), quality assurance (QA) and Total Quality Management (TQM) — see p82-83 for more on these.

Designers do market research to find out what customers want. See p107.

Consumer protection *keeps us safe from dodgy products*

Manufacturers who produce unsafe or unreliable products may be prosecuted under several different laws and regulations.

1) The Trade Descriptions Acts ensure that any claims made about a product (e.g. that it is hard-wearing, long-lasting, waterproof) must be true.
2) The Consumer Safety Act legislates over fire regulations and specifications for clothing, toys, electrical goods, etc.
3) The Sale Of Goods Act ensures that products perform as you would expect and that goods last a reasonable length of time.
4) Fire Safety Regulations cover new and second-hand furniture, stuffed furnishings and fabrics, to ensure resistance to ignition and low toxicity fumes.

As well as the law, consumers can get help from:

1. The Office of Fair Trading
2. The British Standards Institution
3. The Environmental Health Department
4. Local Authority Trading Standards Officers
5. Local Authority Consumer Protection Departments

These places give advice on consumer matters:

1. The Citizens' Advice Bureau
2. The Consumers' Advice Council
3. The National Federation of Consumer Groups
4. The National Consumer Council

Consumer satisfaction should be the aim of all manufacturers

There are quite a few organisations and Acts mentioned here — you need to be familiar with the names of all of them. Know the four main legal acts and some examples of the other helpful bodies.

Consumers

Labels let customers know that the product they've bought is safe and of a good quality. They also help to ensure that the customer is able to get the most out of their product.

Labels tell consumers what's safe

Safety labelling is important to consumers.

Official labels show that standards have been met for safety, quality or design.

These are awarded by the British Standards Institution (BSI) *(their label is the Kitemark)*, the British Electrotechnical Approvals Board (BEAB) or the British Toy and Hobby Manufacturers' Association (BTMA).

If the product is to be sold within the EU, it also must be marked "CE" to show that it meets Central European Standards.

Labels also help consumers **use** and **maintain** a product

1) They can give useful safety instructions.

e.g. "this way up",
"ensure catch is fully locked before use"
"danger — this part gets extremely hot during use"

2) Or they can give maintenance instructions.

e.g. "clean with warm water only",
"do not use abrasives",
"oil frequently"
"do not immerse in water"

Clear labelling is vital if the product is to be used properly

When you do your design and manufacturing project, you need to take all this into account. That includes putting all the right labels on and knowing the appropriate laws and safety codes.

The Environment

Humans exploit and use up the Earth's non-renewable resources simply by using so much stuff. We pollute the water and air and produce large quantities of waste.

The material you choose matters to the environment

1) The rainforests are a prime example of a threatened resource. They produce valuable and exotic hardwoods which are being cut down, but not being replaced. Softwoods (which can regenerate themselves in a person's lifetime) are a greener choice, as are recycled materials that use waste wood, e.g. chipboard. There are sustainable hardwood plantations in some countries, but it costs money to organise them and to check that they're all above board.
2) Metal ores are taken from the Earth's crust. There's only a limited amount of each ore.
3) Most plastics come from oil, which will eventually run out.
4) Recycling and using recycled products is environmentally responsible.
5) Energy efficiency is not only 'green', but cost-effective, too. Manufacturing processes need to be chosen for energy efficiency. If manufacturers wanted to be very responsible, they'd try to use renewable energy sources like wind power or hydroelectricity. This is important when choosing where to site a factory.

Throwing away old products causes pollution

1) At the end of its life, an old product needs to be disposed of to make way for a new one. Most waste goes into landfill sites. Some chemicals used in products cause serious problems when they get into watercourses or into the soil. There are laws about what can be dumped into landfill sites — and what has to be recycled or specially treated to make it safe.
2) Britain's recycling rate stands at 11% — which is about a quarter of what some of its North European neighbours manage. By 2016 EU law will force Britain to cut down to 22% the 80% of it's waste which is currently going into landfill.
3) Packaging contributes to the problem of waste. Designers need to assess how much packaging is actually needed for a product, and how it will be disposed of or recycled.

Think about the amount of packaging on the products you buy

The problem is that the cheapest and most attractive materials and methods of production are not always the most environmentally-friendly. This is what makes being 'green' such a tough battle.

The Environment

Audits and assessments check environmental impact

1) Industry measures waste, emissions and by-products as part of environmental audits.
2) Life cycle assessments evaluate the environmental impact of a product from design brief to disposal of the used product. Every step along the way is analysed.

Designers can adapt products to be more environmentally-friendly

Three examples of environmentally-friendly design — all to do with laundry:

1) Biological washing powders use enzyme technology to enable them to wash clothes at lower temperatures, producing an energy saving of nearly a third.
2) The latest washing machines have forward-tilting drums which require less water to get the clothes wet — and therefore less energy to heat the water up.
3) Some industrial washing machines have polypropylene drums, which are cheaper than using stainless steel. And they're still 'green' because, like steel, the polypropylene can be recycled instead of being scrapped at the end of the drum's life.

Unfortunately recycled products don't always sell well

- Balancing consumer demands against environmental concerns can be difficult.
- Recycling can be more expensive than using fresh materials, and the cost needs to be got back by raising the price of the product.
- Also some recycled products aren't of such high quality as non-recycled ones.

Make sure you know some examples of environmentally-friendly designs

It's a bit of an eye-opener — only 11% of our rubbish is recycled.
But whether environmentalism is an issue that concerns you or not, you still need to learn it.

Warm-Up and Worked Exam Questions

This mini-section is all about thinking how the product will be used in the real world and all the relevant factors that you need to consider. It's interesting stuff, but you do need to think a bit more.

Warm-up Questions

1) What does "ergonomics" mean?
2) Name four social and environmental factors that manufacturers should take into consideration when they are selecting materials, components and manufacturing processes.
3) What are the Trade Descriptions Acts about?
4) How much of Britain's waste is currently going into landfill sites?
5) Give an example of environmentally friendly design in the context of laundry.

Worked Exam Question

I'm afraid this helpful blue writing won't be there in the exam so if I were you I'd make the most of it and make sure you fully understand it now.

1 The diagram below shows a shelf unit, made from hardwood.

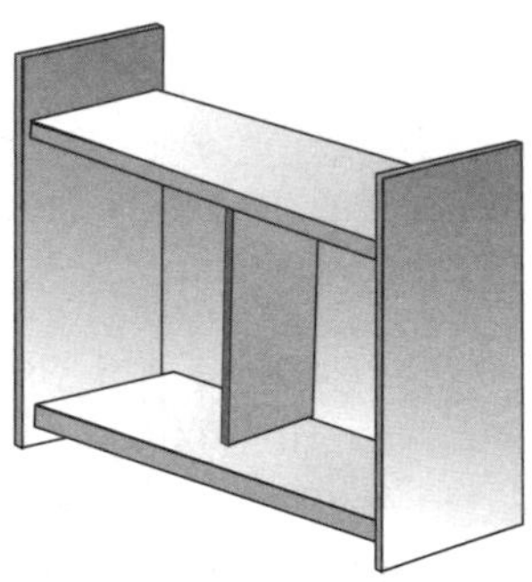

(a) The shelf unit could be made from softwood instead.
Describe **one** advantage to the environment of using softwood instead of hardwood.

Most softwood species grow relatively quickly, regenerating themselves within a person's lifetime. Hardwoods are not so easily replaced as they are much slower growing.

(2 marks)

You're being asked to compare softwoods with hardwoods — so make sure you mention them both.

(b) The shelf unit could be made from chipboard rather than solid wood. Chipboard can be made from recycled waste wood. Give **two** ways in which using recycled waste wood can be an advantage to the environment.

1 *Recycling materials places less of a demand on natural resources.*

2 *The waste material doesn't have to be disposed of, e.g. into landfill sites.*

(2 marks)

Remember that environmental factors are important when you're making a product, and when you're using and disposing of it.

Exam Questions

2 The diagram below shows a symbol found on the labels and packaging of products.

(a) Name the organisation that uses this symbol.

....

(1 mark)

(b) Give an advantage to the consumer of buying a product bearing this symbol.

....

....

(1 mark)

3 (a) Explain what is meant by ergonomic design.

....

....

(2 marks)

(b) Explain how anthropometric data would be used in the design of a chair.

....

....

(2 marks)

(c) Other than chair design, give another example of a product that would benefit from ergonomic design.

....

(1 mark)

Health and Safety

Safety is essential for the person making the product, and the person using the product. The person making the product is responsible for finding out the hazards, and taking action to minimise the risks.

*Wear the right **clothing** ...*

Always wear appropriate protective clothing:

1) While working, especially with machine tools, make sure your sleeves are rolled back, apron ties are tucked in and if you've got long hair, it's tied back.
2) Protect yourself from hazardous material by wearing strong protective gloves.
3) If material is hot, wear protective gloves, an apron and a face mask.
4) Wear goggles or a face mask if using hazardous materials or if a lot of dust or vapours are involved — and make sure there's adequate ventilation.
5) When casting, workers always wear thick all-body suits, face visors, gauntlets and spats (to protect shoes and feet).

*...be careful with **tools** and **machinery**...*

1) Use the safety guards on lathes and drilling machines.
2) Remove chuck keys from chucks before switching on.
3) Make sure you know where the EMERGENCY STOP buttons are, and only use them when needed.
4) Never adjust a machine unless you've switched it off and isolated it first.
5) Never leave machines unattended while switched on.
6) Always secure work safely — e.g. you should clamp work securely for drilling.
7) Don't use machines or hand tools unless you have been shown how.
8) Ensure that any dust extraction equipment is connected and working properly.
9) Carry tools safely.
10) Never operate machines unless allowed to, and under supervision where appropriate.

Chucks and Chuck Keys...
A chuck key is one of those things you use to tighten a drill bit holder (a chuck).
You get chucks on various tools.

...basically, just be careful

1) Don't run or move quickly around the workshop.
2) Never throw anything across the workshop.
3) Be tidy — put tools away when not in use.
4) Report any accidents, faults or breakages to your teacher immediately.
5) Speak up if you see someone else behaving dangerously in the workshop.

Learn this page — it'll help you avoid horrific injury

Safety rules are mainly common sense — but that's no excuse for not learning them. Remember two key points — "identify hazards" and "minimise risks".

Health and Safety

Handle materials and waste sensibly

1) Choose your materials sensibly (only use hazardous materials where necessary).
2) Be careful when carrying heavy or large materials — lift things properly.
3) Make sure materials are safe to handle. Deburr metal (file down any rough edges) before you start work.
4) Beware of naked flames or red-hot heating elements — and keep them away from flammable liquids.
5) Make sure you dispose of waste properly (this is also an environmental issue — see p90-91).
6) When storing material, make sure it's put away safely so it can't fall or slide and injure anyone.
7) Never clear away metal shavings/dust with your bare hands — use a brush.

Design safe products — think about the consumer

When designing products, think 'safety'. Products which may harm the end user are generally inappropriate. Sometimes it's impossible to avoid potential harm completely (e.g. sharp tools), but for these products effort should be made to at least minimise the risks.

> Safety is also important for the consumer.
> People don't want to risk death every time they boil the kettle.

1) Products should have any unnecessary sharp corners and edges smoothed so that consumers can't cut themselves. (This includes any attachments — e.g. attaching the eyes of a teddy bear by 10 cm metal spikes would be a thoroughly bad and unsafe idea.)
2) Toys often end up in children's mouths, so don't finish the surface with any toxic paint or varnish. Check this out at the research stage and choose a non-toxic range of surface treatments.
3) Small components must be firmly attached so that a young child can't pull them off — this would be a choking hazard. (Toys with detachable components would be unsuitable for small children.)
4) Use standard components wherever you can, because these have already been rigorously tested by the manufacturer — this helps make sure that safety standards are met.

A bad reputation can cause companies serious damage

They can get sued, or people can just stop buying their products. Taking health and safety precautions in your our own project is about protecting yourself, your work mates, and the consumers.

Health and Safety

There are a number of organisations and laws that aim to minimise health and safety risks during manufacture. You need to know the ones listed here. You also need to make sure that you apply these standards to your own work in the workshop.

There are **laws** on health and safety

1) To protect consumers, there are safety standards applied to many products by the British Standards Institute (BSI). Products which meet these standards are awarded the Kitemark (see p89). Manufacturers usually incorporate this in their label. Many plastic products have it moulded on.

2) The Health and Safety at Work Act and COSHH (Control Of Substances Hazardous to Health) relate to safety in the workplace. They're designed to protect you from hazardous (mainly chemical) products or dangerous working practices which may pose a risk to your health.

Risk assessment is important for workers and consumers

1) Risk assessment is a procedure which is carried out to identify and minimise any potential risks of using chemicals, machinery or equipment. It may also be carried out on a product to highlight any potential risk to the end user and ensure precautions are taken to minimise potential danger.

2) Employers, workshop managers and your technology teacher must assess the risks involved in using workshop facilities and justify the level of precaution taken, e.g. placing warning or caution signs on machines, installing non-slip flooring or erecting barriers and guards.

Choose a piece of machinery you use in school and ask yourself these questions:

1) What could go wrong?
2) What effect would this have?
3) What can I do to prevent it happening?
4) What system could I implement to make sure the risk is minimised?

ALWAYS make sure you're working to safety standards

Risk assessment comes down to working out what might go wrong and preventing it going wrong. Toys are a good example of safety in design — kids put things in their mouths... potentially disastrous.

Warm-Up and Worked Exam Questions

Safety has to be considered throughout the whole process — to avoid accidents during manufacture and to make sure that the final product meets required safety standards. There's a lot of rules and laws on these pages that you should learn. Test how much you've remembered with these questions...

Warm-up Questions

1) List 3 safety rules relating to clothing that should be followed in appropriate situations.
2) List 3 safety rules relating to the use of machinery.
3) List 3 safety rules relating to the handling of materials and waste.
4) How should you make a rough-edged piece of metal safe to handle?
5) In the context of safety laws, what does COSHH stand for?
6) What is risk assessment? Give two situations in which it should be carried out.

You need to take Health and Safety issues very seriously — not just for your own safety, but because you could easily get a question on it...

Worked Exam Question

1 (a) The diagram below is a safety warning sign.

What is the meaning of the safety sign?

Safety goggles must be worn.

(1 mark)

(b) Give three safety precautions that should be taken when using machine tools.

1 *Tie back long hair.*

(1 mark)

2 *Find out where the emergency stop button is.*

(1 mark)

3 *Make sure your work is secured safely.*

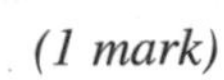

(1 mark)

There are lots of other things you could say for this, e.g. removing chuck keys, using safety guards on lathes or drilling machines — they're all on page 94.

Exam Questions

2 Other than safety goggles, give four items of protective clothing that may be worn when working with machine tools.

1 ....

(1 mark)

2 ....

(1 mark)

3 ....

(1 mark)

4 ....

(1 mark)

3 Briefly describe the process of risk assessment.

....

....

(2 marks)

4 The diagram below shows a toy car which is being produced for children aged 2-4.

(a) It has been decided that the wheels should be firmly attached. Why is this an important safety consideration?

....

....

(2 marks)

(b) Explain one other important safety consideration that should be taken into account in the design of the car.

....

....

(2 marks)

Revision Summary for Section Five

You can't go just yet. You have to do these questions first, to check you've learnt everything in this section. Think of it as Learning Quality Control.

1) Why do you need to do product analysis?
2) What are form and function?
3) Name five other factors that you should look at when analysing a product.
4) What is quality assurance?
5) What are tolerances?
6) If a component had to be 35 mm ± 0.2 mm, what would be the upper and lower tolerances? Would 34.7 mm be OK?
7) Give an example of non-destructive testing.
8) Do you need to do quality control on your own work?
9) If you were being environmentally responsible, what kind of material might you choose for a disposable product?
10) What is ergonomics?
11) What's the technical name for body measurement data?
12) What sort of impact can a badly designed product have on the user's health?
13) What are the Trade Descriptions Acts about?
14) What is the Sale of Goods Act for?
15) Whose symbol is the Kitemark? What do they do?
16) Name three types of information you might find on a product label.
17) Give an example of a maintenance/safety label that you might see on a hand-held electric blender.
18) Name two non-renewable resources.
19) Give three examples of ways that manufacturers and designers can reduce the environmental impact of a product.
20) How does packaging affect the environment?
21) What is a life cycle assessment of a product?
22) Where should a chuck key be before you operate a drill?
23) If you see someone breaking safety rules in the workshop, what should you do?
24) When should you wear goggles? (In the context of D&T.)
25) Why are small removable parts inappropriate to use on toys for very small children?
26) Why must surface treatments on toys be non-toxic?
27) What is COSHH?
28) What is risk assessment? Who does it?

Scale of Production

The term 'scale of production' is all about the quantity of products that you're going to manufacture. Commercially there are four main categories for you to learn.

Jobbing production — making a *one-off* product

1) This is where you're making a single product.
2) Every item made will be different, to meet the customer's individual and specific requirements.
3) This type of production is very labour intensive, and requires a highly skilled workforce.
4) Examples are wide-ranging, from made-to-measure furniture to one-off buildings like the Millennium Dome.

Hand-made furniture is often tailored to suit the client

Fitted Kitchens are produced to meet the individual needs of the customer

Batch production — making a *specific quantity* of a product

1) This is where you're making a specific quantity of a particular product.
2) Batches can be repeated as many times as required.
3) The machinery and labour used need to be flexible, so they can quickly change from making a batch of one type of product to making another batch of a different but similar product.
4) The time between batches, when machines and tools may have to be set up differently or changed around, is called down time. This is unproductive and needs to be kept as short as possible so the manufacturer doesn't lose money.

Examples of products suited to batch production

Down time is BAD because it's unproductive — nothing is being manufactured

One-off products are expensive and slow to make. Batch produced products are cheaper and you can create lots more in the same length of time. Both methods require a certain sort of workforce.

Scale of Production

Mass *production —* ***high-volume*** *production*

1) Mass production means making products on a really large scale, such as cars or electrical goods.
2) It often uses expensive specialised equipment including Computer-Aided Manufacture (CAM) and industrial robots.
3) As well as all this equipment, you need a large workforce. The different stages of production and manufacture are broken down into simple repetitive tasks which people are able to learn easily.
4) Recruitment is relatively easy — you don't need to employ skilled people.

Continuous *production —* ***non-stop*** *production 24hrs/day*

1) This involves non-stop, uninterrupted production.
2) The specialised equipment required costs so much that it would be too expensive to turn it off. So it has to keep running and producing continuously.
3) Examples of continuous production include oil and chemical manufacture.

Which category *do I use in the* ***school*** *workshop?*

If you're making a single product that you've designed, with its own specification, it will be jobbing production.

Sometimes you may work with the rest of the class in small teams, all making different parts of a product which you then bring together and assemble to produce a number of identical products. This will be batch production.

It's not what you've got — it's how much of it you've got

High volumes mean you can't afford skilled people, and you can't let them spend much time on things. Maintaining the quality is difficult, so breaking the tasks right down means everything can be monitored.

Manufacturing Systems

These two pages show you the five main manufacturing systems. Learn how they work.

Cell production is working in teams to produce components

1) Production stages are split into individual components, which are each made by a different production cell.

2) Each cell has a team of people working to produce a single component.

3) Within each cell the team is responsible for all aspects of production, including quality control and maintenance of the machines.

4) Advantages of this method include teamwork, communication and quality.

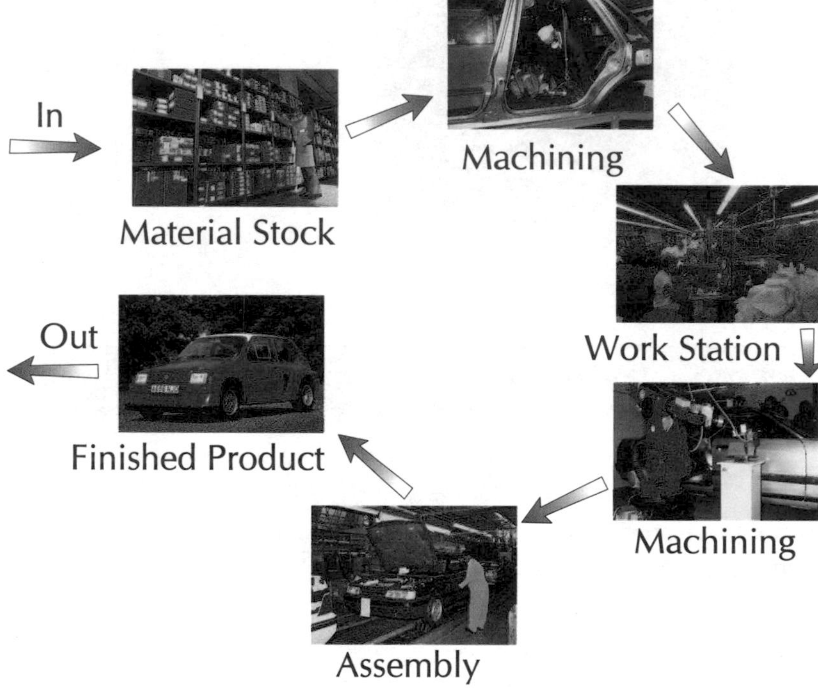

In-line assembly is used for mass production

1) Most of the production line is automated.

2) Unskilled labour is used mainly for assembly, with a small number of semi-skilled operators making sure there's a continuous flow along the production line.

3) A disadvantage of this system is the lack of flexibility when compared with cells.

Cell production — small, modular teams of workers

Cell production is actually quite a "nice" way of working — the workers feel they are jointly responsible for the overall quality of the product. This can be quite a motivating factor.

Manufacturing Systems

These systems are basically about making the production process as efficient as possible. It's common sense really — different manufacturing systems are more appropriate for different companies and products. There's no 'perfect' manufacturing system.

Flexible manufacturing systems use **semi-skilled** workers

1) The FMS approach is based on the belief that the key to successful manufacturing is a flexible workforce and flexible machinery.
2) Individual people are semi-skilled, being able to do a variety of jobs.
3) It works well with batch production, where change and flexibility are essential.

Concurrent engineering needs **good communication**

1) This is where different stages of the design process can overlap (one can start work before the other has finished) — which saves time.

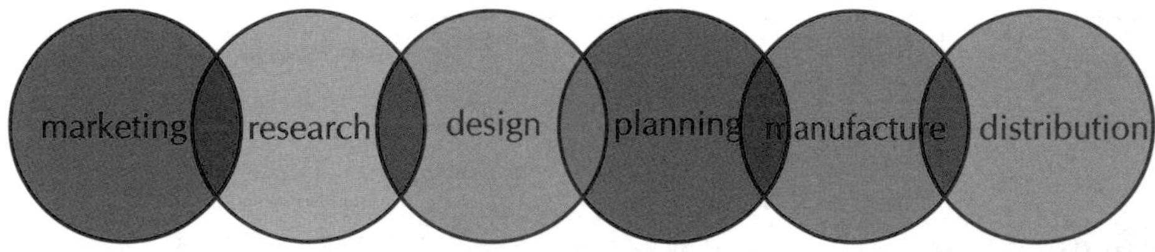

2) It's essential to make sure there are good communication links between all the stages of the design process, e.g. marketing, research, design, planning, manufacture and distribution.
3) The overall aim is to design and make the product with maximum efficiency.

Just-in-time manufacturing needs detailed **forward planning**

1) For just-in-time manufacture (JIT), you only buy materials and components as and when you need them.
2) This removes the need for large stockpiles of resources, saving money and space.
3) Everything has to be kept on time, or things can easily go wrong.

Just-in-time manufacturing can be quite a risky business

Only two pages on this topic. And this is useful stuff — especially if you go anywhere near the manufacturing industry when you leave school. Even if not, you still have to learn it for your GCSEs.

Warm-Up and Worked Exam Questions

More real-world stuff in this section — now it's about understanding all the different ways that real products are manufactured. It's interesting, but it's also more facts to test yourself on...

Warm-up Questions

1) What is jobbing production?
2) Which requires a more skilled workforce, batch production or mass production?
3) Why should "down time" be kept short?
4) Give two examples of continuous production.
5) How does cell production work?
6) In which manufacturing system do stages of the design process overlap?
7) What is JIT manufacturing?

You may be getting tired of exam questions by now, but this is the last section with questions (before the practice exam), so don't worry — the end is in sight.

Worked Exam Question

1 Complete the table below by naming or describing each type of production. The first one has been done for you.

Type of Production	Description
Mass production	Products are manufactured on a large scale. Production is broken down into simple repetitive tasks.
Batch production	A specific quantity of a product is made. Machinery and labour needs to be flexible, so they can quickly change to making another, similar product.
Jobbing production	*A highly skilled workforce is used to make one-off products, designed to meet a customer's individual and specific requirements.*
Continuous production	Production is non-stop, with machines operating twenty-four hours a day.

Look at the answers that have been done for you for an indication of how much detail to give.

If you don't know an answer, GUESS. At least you'll have a chance of getting the marks.

(3 marks)

Exam Questions

2 A manufacturer is deciding what manufacturing system to use to make a new product.

(a) One manufacturing system that could be chosen is cell production.

(i) Describe what is meant by cell production.

....

....

(2 marks)

(ii) Give one advantage of cell production.

....

(1 mark)

(b) The manufacturer discovers that it is difficult to recruit skilled or semi-skilled workers within the local area, but that there is a ready supply of unskilled workers.

(i) Name two production systems that would not be suitable for an unskilled workforce.

1 ....

(1 mark)

2 ....

(1 mark)

(ii) Explain why mass production can mainly be carried out by unskilled workers.

....

....

(2 marks)

(c) In just-in-time manufacturing, materials and components are bought as and when they are needed. Give one advantage and one disadvantage of just-in-time manufacture.

Advantage:

....

(1 mark)

Disadvantage:

....

(1 mark)

Advertising and Marketing

In industry, just making something isn't good enough — you've got to be able to sell it.

There are five key roles in the design process

A product developed for industry not only needs to work, and fulfil its design purpose — it also needs to make a profit. Along the way, there are key people who have important roles to play:

1) Client — identifies a need, gives the designer a clear brief, carries out market research and raises money for the project.
2) Designer — develops the client's ideas, sets out a specification and produces detailed working drawings of the final design.
3) Manufacturer — plans and carries out manufacturing, safely and efficiently, to produce consistent results and make a profit.
4) Retailer — gives customers what they want, at an affordable price.
5) User — gets a high quality product that works, fulfils a need and is good value for money.

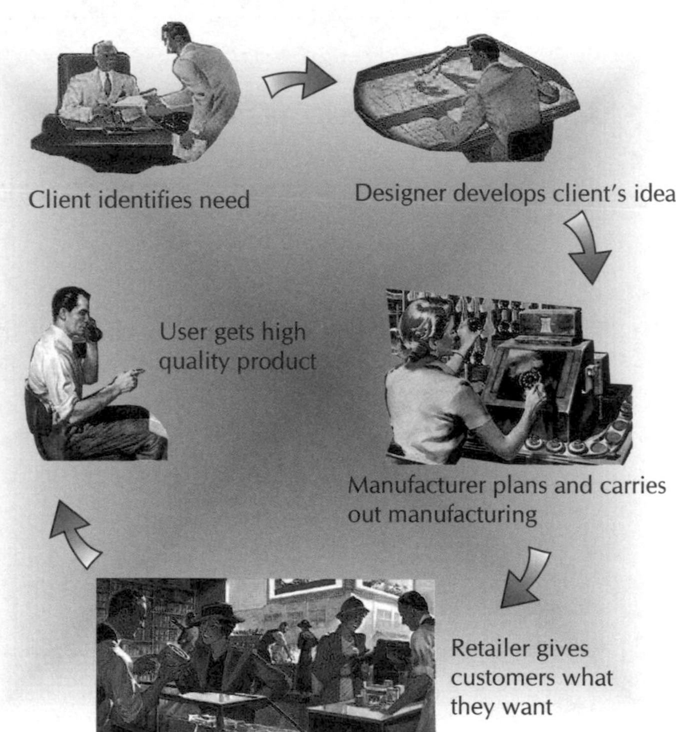

Legislation — BSI and ISO

1) BSI — the British Standards Institution is a quality control organisation. It sets out standards, testing procedures and quality assurance techniques.
2) Kitemark — any product meeting BSI standards is given a Kitemark, as long as the manufacturer can ensure all their products are of the same standard.

3) ISO 9000 — the ISO 9000 is an internationally agreed set of standards (see p82).
4) Drawing conventions — the ISO standards give specific ways of drawing things (e.g. circuit diagrams), so that anyone looking at a standardised drawing can read it in the same way.

Learn the five key roles

Five key roles in the design process, a few details and four numbered points about legislation — close the book, write it all down and keep going till you don't miss any details.

Advertising and Marketing

You need marketing to find out what people want, and to convince them that they want your product.

There are **two** main types of **marketing**

1) ADVERTISING MEDIA — advertising media include newspapers, magazines, mail, television, radio, cinema, posters, e-mail and the Internet. All advertising aims to influence people, and convince people to buy a product.

2) MARKET RESEARCH — this is often useful to find out who your customers are and what their needs are. It can be carried out using published statistics, surveys or questionnaires.

Advertising Standards — the ASA (Advertising Standards Authority) regulates all advertising in the UK. It makes sure that adverts are legal, honest, responsible and fair.

Designing your own **questionnaire**

1) Write your questions carefully, so the answers give you information you can use.
2) Be brief, relevant, clear and inoffensive.
3) Multiple-choice questions are often a good idea.

Tobacco advertising was banned because it was deemed irresponsible

Marketing's such a tricky thing that it's easy to see why companies are so fond of market research. Even if it's a pain in the neck for everyone else who ends up with a doormat covered in junk mail.

Warm-Up and Worked Exam Questions

Marketing — another interesting topic if you ask me. We've definitely saved the best 'til last. But whether you like it or not, there's still some questions here — you know what you have to do...

Warm-up Questions

1) What does BSI stand for?
2) What is ISO 9000?
3) What is an advertising media? Give five examples of advertising media.
4) What does the Advertising Standards Authority do?
5) What advice would you give someone who was writing questions for a market research questionnaire?

Worked Exam Question

Imagine if you opened up your exam paper and all the answers were already written in for you. Hmm, well I'm afraid that's not going to happen, the only way you'll do well is hard work now.

1 Companies carry out marketing in order to make sure their product sells.

(a) One main type of marketing is advertising. Why might companies choose to advertise their products?

Advertising aims to influence people and persuade them to buy their product.

There's no strict right answer, so use your common sense.

(1 mark)

(b) Name four advertising media.
The first one has been done for you.

1 Radio

2 *Newspapers*

3 *Television*

4 *Posters*

(3 marks)

(b) Other than advertising, name and describe another type of marketing.

Name: *Market research*

Description: *Used to find out who the customers are and what their needs are. It can be carried out using published statistics, surveys or questionnaires.*

(3 marks)

You need to give two marks worth of information here — the answer doesn't just say what market research is for, it says how you do it too.

Exam Questions

2 There are various key roles in the design process.

(a) Fill in the missing roles in the table below, to show how a product progresses from client to user.

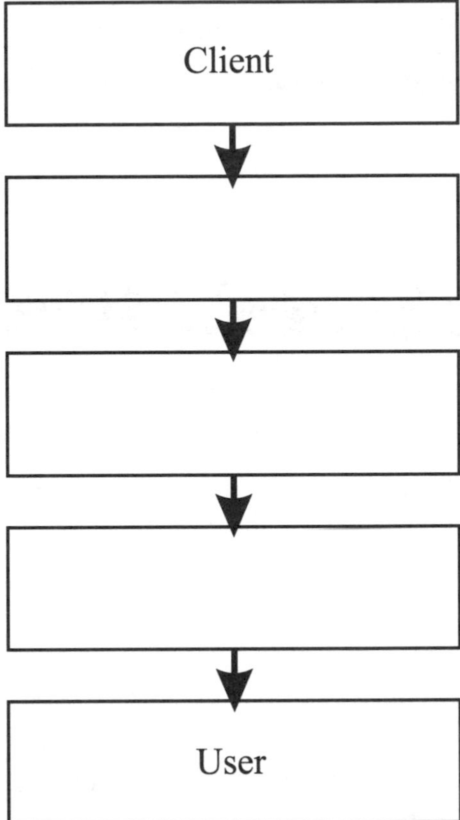

(3 marks)

(b) Choose one of the roles from the above table, and briefly describe their part in the design process.

Role: ....

Description: ....

....

(2 marks)

Good Working Practice

In school, good working practice is all about forward planning and organisation.
In industry it means pretty much the same thing — it's just done on a much larger scale.

Quality control — controlling the quality of a product

See p82 for more stuff on QC.

1) Quality control is easy to include and monitor in any project if you build it into a flow chart.
2) Many of the questions / decisions (diamond symbols) will form quality control points automatically.

Flow charts — project planning using symbols

1) A flow chart is a simple diagram showing the order that things happen in (also see p8). It works just as well for a simple school project or for a complex manufacturing process.
2) There are standard symbols used, so that once you know the basics you'll be able to read and understand any flow chart. All the shapes are linked with simple arrows, which guide the reader through the chart.

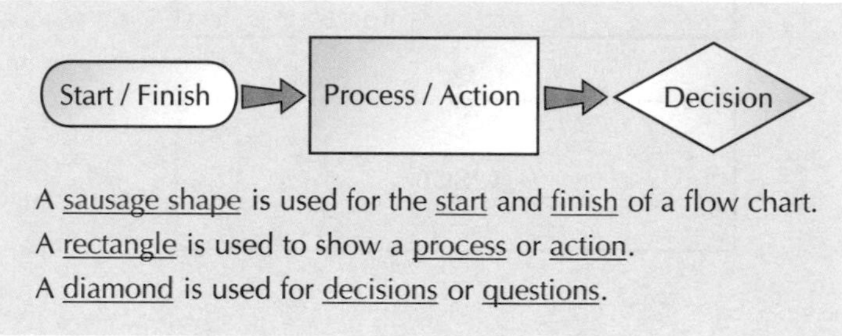

A sausage shape is used for the start and finish of a flow chart.
A rectangle is used to show a process or action.
A diamond is used for decisions or questions.

3) Often small sections of a project have their own flow chart, to avoid any single chart getting too complicated. A summary chart can be used to give an overview of the whole project, leaving the details of each section for the smaller charts.
4) Splits or loops in a flow chart are important when questions need to be asked. If you're including a question, think about all the possible answers, and where these will lead you on the flow chart.

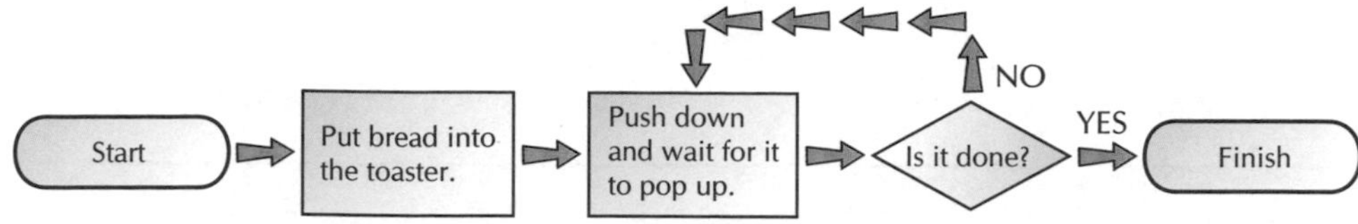

Flowcharts make life much easier

This is a good technique for your own project. If your process has loads of little stages, it's best to summarise them in one big flowchart, then have the finer details in separate, smaller, flowcharts.

Good Working Practice

Good working practice is about making the most of the time you have when you're making a product. You need to be realistic about the time it takes to do tasks when you're planning the production processes. You could end up having to plan your project all over again, or running out of time completely.

Time planning means forward thinking

1) Good planning is often just a question of thinking ahead. What will need to be done in a project and in what order?

2) One example of a planning tool is a Gantt chart (also see p8). This is a table where you plot activities or stages in a project against time.

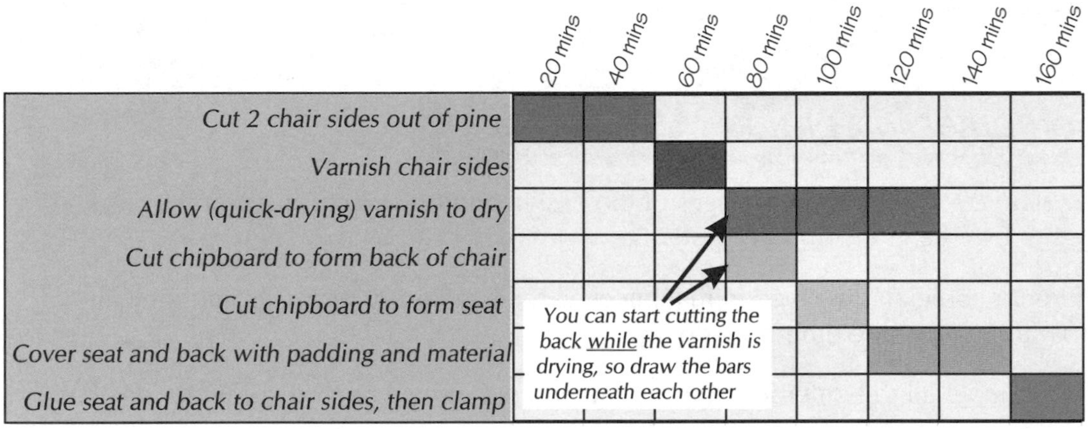

	20 mins	40 mins	60 mins	80 mins	100 mins	120 mins	140 mins	160 mins
Cut 2 chair sides out of pine								
Varnish chair sides								
Allow (quick-drying) varnish to dry								
Cut chipboard to form back of chair								
Cut chipboard to form seat								
Cover seat and back with padding and material								
Glue seat and back to chair sides, then clamp								

You can start cutting the back while the varnish is drying, so draw the bars underneath each other

3) If realistic time limits are set at the start, then you can use the chart to monitor your progress through a project. The marked out areas can be shaded in as they're completed.

4) Some stages on a Gantt chart will overlap, meaning that you can start one section before the previous section is finished.

5) Other stages will not overlap — instead they will simply run one after another.

Always plan ahead — a good lesson for manufacturing

These charts are also handy for your own project. The main trick is to keep them up to date. They're no use at all if you set them up at the beginning, then don't look at them again until you've finished.

CAD/CAM and CIM in Industry

All this computer-aided stuff is here to make life easier for everyone. You need to learn what all the abbreviations mean, and how these processes are useful in industry.

CAD/CAM — Computer-Aided Design and Manufacture

1) CAD (Computer-Aided Design) is all about using computers to help design a product.
2) CAM (Computer-Aided Manufacture) refers to any part of the manufacturing process that's controlled by a computer system.
3) CAD/CAM (Computer-Aided Design and Manufacture) is the process of joining CAD and CAM systems together. This involves the use of specialised computer software that converts data from drawings into machining instructions.

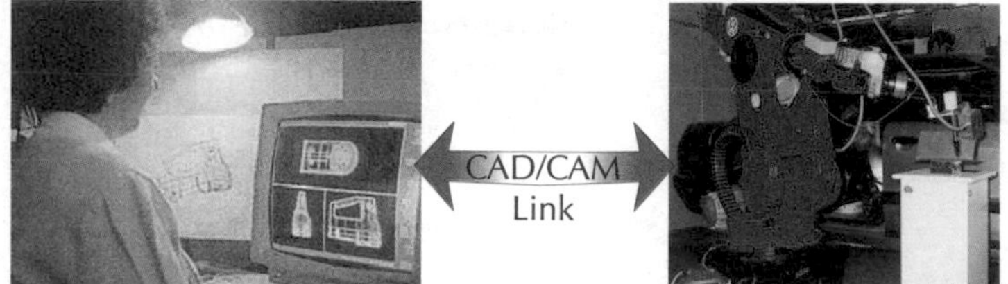

CIM — Computer-Integrated Manufacturing

1) CIM is the system by which different stages of the design and manufacturing process are linked together by a central computer system.
2) A lot of different people are involved in making even the simplest of products and they all need to be aware of what the others are doing.
3) CIM helps coordinate all the different stages in the process using a central computer database.
4) With this system no stage is carried out in isolation, as communication is made easy through the central computer system.
5) The really clever bit is the software held on the central computer. It will automatically update any changes made and alert all the related stages. For example if a change is made in a CAD program, the software will automatically change the corresponding CNC program that controls the manufacturing machines. This can save a lot of time and eliminate some costly mistakes.

Summary of Abbreviations

1) CAD — Computer-Aided Design — designing on the computer.
2) CAM — Computer-Aided Manufacture — using a computer to control the machines making the product.
3) CAD/CAM — Computer-Aided Design & Manufacture — links CAD & CAM.
4) CIM — Computer-Integrated Manufacturing — links many different stages of the designing and manufacturing process.
5) CNC — Computer Numerical Control — runs computer-controlled machines.

Learn all the details

This computer controlled stuff really is quite clever. Learn all the numbered points then write a mini-essay explaining how CAD/CAM and CIM work, to check you've got all the points covered.

Jigs, Moulds and Templates

Jigs, moulds and templates are pretty handy things all round — they save you a lot of work. In industry they're used to increase the speed and efficiency of the production process.

Templates are used to make repetitive shapes

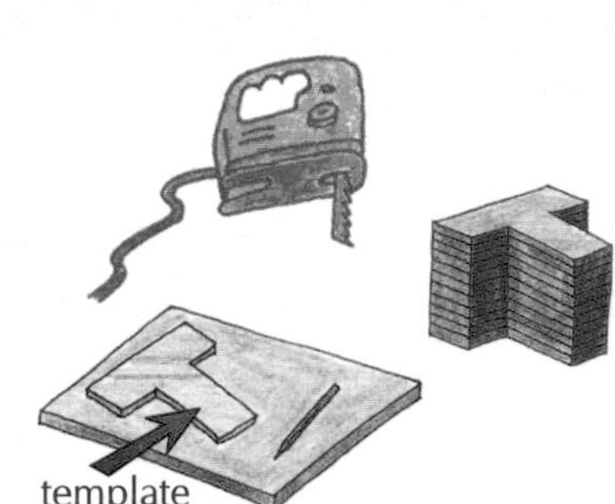

1) Templates are very easy to make and simple to use.
2) You can use them to reproduce any number of identical shapes from one original pattern (template). The original is used to draw, scribe or cut round.
3) Templates need to be strong and hard-wearing so that they can be used repetitively without wearing down.
4) Afterwards, the components can be checked against the templates for accuracy.

Jigs help manufacture repetitive components

1) A jig guides the tools that are working on a component.
2) Jigs come in many different shapes and sizes and can be specifically made for a particular job.

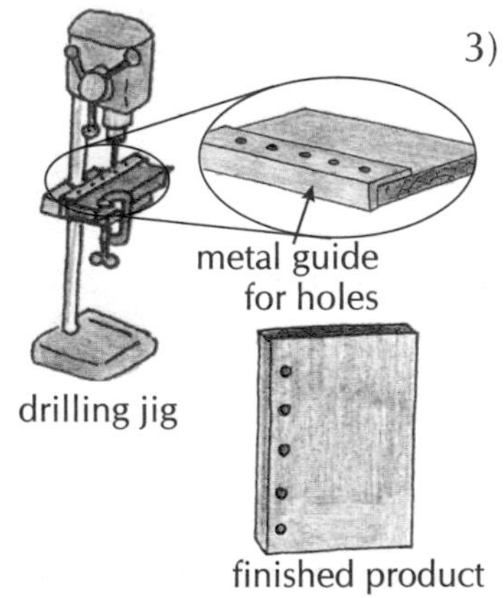

3) They're designed to speed up production and simplify the making process.
4) A drilling jig gets rid of the need for complex marking out. It can also help cut down on errors, and make sure every component is identical.
5) Some jigs are a standard size and shape and could be used on many different jobs. E.g. a dovetail jig enables complex dovetail joints (see p30) to be machined with a router, very quickly and easily, and with minimal measuring and marking out.

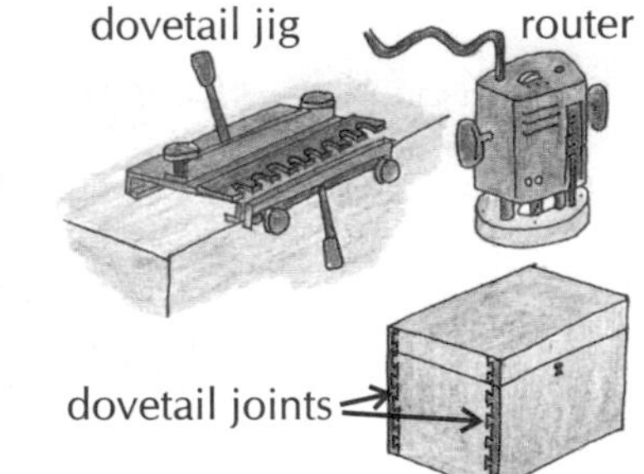

Moulds are used to reproduce 3-D shapes

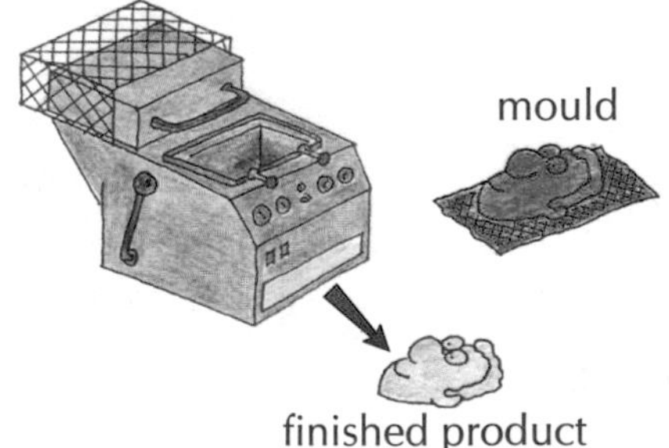

1) Moulds are most commonly used in plastics manufacturing, in processes such as vacuum forming, compression moulding and blow moulding. See p21-23 for more on moulding.
2) Once an accurate mould has been made, detailed plastic shapes can be formed with it over and over again.
3) Industrial moulds are expensive to produce, so a manufacturer needs to be certain of their design, and needs to be able to make large numbers of their product to make it cost-effective.

Design your own jigs, moulds and templates

As part of your GCSE project, you could design and make very simple jigs, moulds or templates to help you produce some of your components. By doing this you will also be able to illustrate how, in theory, you could put your product into small-scale batch production.

It's all about Speed and Quality Control

I suggest you learn how this all saves time in industry and how it could be used to improve your project. Start by learning the subheadings, then start to fill in the details.

Warm-Up and Worked Exam Questions

Take your time to go through this — the final mini-section of questions. If any of the facts are baffling you it's not too late to take another peek over the section.

Warm-up Questions

1) Draw a flow chart for the process of washing the dishes.
2) What does it mean if two sections on a Gantt chart overlap?
3) What does CIM stand for?
4) Describe what CIM is.
5) What is a template, and how is it used?
6) What's the difference between a mould and a template?

This is the last set of exam questions before the practice exam.
So make an extra big effort with these ones and do us proud.

Worked Exam Question

1 This question is about using computers in design and manufacture.

(a) Companies are increasingly using CAM in industry.

(i) What does CAM stand for?

Computer-aided manufacture.

(1 mark)

Make sure you don't give the same answer as (a)(i) — they're asking you to describe what it is.

(ii) Give a brief description of what is meant by CAM.

CAM is using computers to control any part of the manufacturing process.

(1 mark)

(b) CAD stands for Computer-Aided Design.

(i) What is meant by CAD/CAM?

CAD/CAM is the linking of computer-aided design with computer-aided manufacture.

(1 marks)

(ii) How could the use of CAD/CAM increase the profitability of a product?

By linking CAD and CAM into one system, the whole process of design and manufacture can be controlled as a whole, saving time and eliminating mistakes.

(2 marks)

This is basically asking how CAD/CAM helps to save money during the manufacturing process.

Exam Questions

2 The diagram below shows a table which is to be produced in a batch of 2000.

The edge of the table top is decorated with a series of holes.
A jig is to be used to assist the drilling of these holes.

(a) Explain how using a jig can make production more efficient.

....

....

(2 marks)

(b) In the space below, draw a jig that you would use in drilling the holes.
Include notes on the drawing to explain how the jig would be used.

(6 marks)

Revision Summary for Section Six

There's a lot of important stuff in this section, so you need to revise it well. You can be sure that there'll always be an exam question on some area of 'Industrial Awareness'. Try these questions again and again until you know all the important facts and details off by heart.

1) Give a simple definition of "scale of production". What are the 4 main types?
2) How many products would you make at a time in jobbing production?
3) What type of production would you use to make a specific quantity of a product?
4) Why, in the above production method, do machinery and labour need to be flexible?
5) a) What is high volume production (e.g. production of cars or electrical goods) called?
   b) How are the tasks broken down, in this type of production and what skill level is needed of the workforce?
6) In continuous production, why do the machines have to run non-stop?
7) Describe cell production, and list 3 advantages of it.
8) Describe in-line assembly, and give one disadvantage of it.
9) What does FMS stand for? What does this approach see as the key to successful manufacturing?
10) Which manufacturing system needs good communication links between stages?
11) What does JIT stand for? What things does it eliminate?
12) Which of the manufacturing systems do you think would be best for making twenty identical wooden bookcases?
13) What are the 5 key roles in the design process? Describe each in detail.
14) What does BSI stand for? Describe what it sets out to do.
15) Sketch a Kitemark and explain what it stands for.
16) What is the ISO 9000? What does it aim to do?
17) Why does part of the ISO outline specific drawing requirements?
18) Which authority regulates all British advertising?
19) Name six types of media which are used for advertising. What's the main purpose of an advert?
20) Why is market research important?
21) If you were designing a questionnaire, how would you structure the questions?
22) What is a flow chart?
23) Sketch the standard symbols used in a flow chart, and explain what each one represents.
24) How can you build quality control into a flow chart? What would it be used for?
25) When would you use a split or loop in a flow chart?
26) What's the point of planning ahead in a project?
27) Sketch a simple example of a Gantt chart, and explain how to use it.
28) What does CAD stand for, and what's it all about?
29) What does CAM stand for? What processes does it refer to?
30) Explain the process of CAD/CAM. What does it involve?
31) Describe CIM. What does it do, and what's the really clever bit?
32) List some of the advantages of using CIM.
33) What is a jig? Why are drilling jigs useful?
34) What are templates used for?

Tips on Getting Started

This section's got all the things that exam boards criticise people for not doing.
Read this before you start your project to make sure you don't throw away marks.

Step 1 — get your idea

You can get ideas from different places — for example, your teacher might:

1) tell you exactly what your task is.
2) give you a range of tasks to choose from.
3) leave the project choice completely up to you.

Don't choose anything too easy or too boring

Choose a project that will:

1) stretch you and let you demonstrate just how good you are. If the project's too easy, or contains little scope for design, then you'll lose valuable marks.
2) be interesting and challenging enough to keep you motivated. Coursework's a long old process, and you need to stay committed.
3) give you the opportunity to produce a wide range of research, and demonstrate your ICT skills.
4) allow for a variety of solutions, resulting in a project which can be completed before the deadline (and this includes allowing time for testing and evaluation).

The design brief — give lots of detail

See page 1 for more on the design brief

1) Your idea needs to have real commercial potential.
2) You need to describe exactly what you're trying to do.
3) Explain all the factors you need to consider — things like price, weight, market trends, etc.

Think hard before you start — you'll regret choosing a dull project...

It might seem like a ridiculous idea, but try and choose a project that doesn't bore you to tears.
You're much more likely to produce higher quality work, and get higher marks.

Tips on Getting Started

You need to be organised and methodical when you're compiling your research. It'll save you a lot of time when you come to writing up your research analysis.

Say why your research is relevant

1) DON'T put bits of paper in your research folder without any explanation.
2) DON'T just copy and paste stuff from the Internet.
3) DO write notes on every piece of research to say why it's relevant, how it changed your thinking or how it backed up your existing ideas.
4) DO refer back to the research section throughout the project — that helps to show that you've used your research.

This is all you need to do:

See page 2 for more on research

Print or photocopy the relevant stuff.

This is my clever and interesting research that I got off the Internet. This is my clever and interesting research that I got off the Internet. This is my clever and interesting research that I got off the Internet. This is my clever and interesting that I got off the Internet. This is my clever and interesting research that I got off the Internet. This is my clever and interesting research that I got off the Internet.

Highlight the really useful bits.

Write brief notes saying where you found it...

...what you found out...

...and what effect it's had on your project.

I found this on the Clever and Interesting Website (www.clever.co.uk).
The highlighted part explains how the cleverness affects the interestingness of products. I hadn't previously considered these effects so I will now incorporate the use of different materials into my testing.

Remember — your research analysis will contain all the conclusions from your research. But these notes will help you write that research analysis, and will also help the examiner understand why you made your decisions.

Three BIG reasons why research is important...

1) It helps you to get started and solidify your ideas 2) Presenting your research well shows the examiners you know what you're doing 3) It helps to direct your project as you go along.

Tips on Development

If you're smart you'll keep planning and evaluating throughout your project.
If you're daft you'll do a bit at the start, then forget about it and get a bad mark for your project.

You need a ***wide range*** *of* ***ideas*** *— be* ***creative***

1) There's always more than one way of doing your project well.

2) Consider plenty of different ways to solve the problem.

3) Don't just come up with one good idea and stick with it.
You'll only be sure it's the best idea if you've thought about other ways of doing it.

4) The examiners do really get annoyed about this one — so get those creative juices flowing.

Developing *your* ***ideas*** *— try out a few* ***alternatives***

1) The same goes for developing ideas as for creating them — there's lots of different things you could do.

2) Once you've got the idea, there are still plenty of ways to turn that into a great product.

Do ***loads*** *of* ***planning*** *— and* ***not just*** *at the* ***start***

Planning affects your whole project, not just the start of it.
These are the things you should do:

OVERALL PROJECT PLAN AT THE START:

1) to help you focus on the task.

2) to make sure you know what stage you should have reached at any time — this way, if you fall behind schedule, you'll know about it as soon as possible, and can do something about it.

3) to allow enough time for all the different stages of the design process — including testing, evaluation, and writing up your project.

PLAN YOUR RESEARCH:

Work out what research you need to do, and how long you're going to allow yourself for each bit (e.g. questionnaires, disassembling a competing product, and so on).

DON'T GET BOGGED DOWN:

When you're generating proposals or developing your product, don't spend too long working on one little aspect of the product. There's a lot to do — so try to keep your project moving forward.

Be realistic about how long things will take you to do

Remember to leave time for testing and evaluation in your time plan. It's all too easy to forget them.

Tips on Evaluation

Evaluation means examining and judging your work (and you have to do this as part of your project — it's not just something for the examiner to do). If your product doesn't work, but you explain why, you can still get good marks.

Test and evaluate your product throughout the project

Quote from one of the Chief Examiners' Reports.

> *"To be achieving the highest marks in this section, candidates must show that they have used a clear and objective testing strategy."*

i.e. it's important.

Don't wait until you're finished to evaluate your work

1) Like any designer, it's a good idea to be thinking about evaluation from the moment you start working on your design brief.
2) Make notes on your designs and developments as you go along, explaining what was good and bad about each one.
3) When you're writing up your final evaluation, you can also think about whether you'd do anything differently if you were starting again. It's okay if you made some bad decisions during your project — everyone does. But you can get marks if you explain why they were bad decisions, and what you wish you'd done instead.

Check your brief and specification

You need to evaluate your product fully. Use these guidelines:

1) Compare your final product to your brief and specification. Does your product satisfy all the conditions it's supposed to? If not, why not?
2) Try to get a likely user (or an expert in this kind of product, maybe) to trial your product and give their honest opinions. This will give you a realistic view of whether it's fit for its purpose — e.g. does it do what it's meant to? And if it does, how well? They may also be able to give you ideas for improvements.
3) It's also really important to think about things you could have done better, such as...

> 1) Time implications — did you spend too much time in one area, or rush to finish?
> 2) Practical work — were you completely satisfied with the quality of your final product?
> 3) Would you approach aspects of your design and development work in a different way?

You can make mistakes and get marks — all at the same time...

Everyone makes mistakes in their D&T projects. So don't worry too much when it happens to you. Just explain what went wrong and how you'd avoid it in the future. You can get marks for that.

Tips on Presentation

It's no use doing a brilliant project if your presentation's poor. You've put a lot of time and effort into your project (probably) so it would be a shame for you to mess it up at the last stage. It really is worth putting in those few extra hours.

Organise your evaluation well

Your evaluation should be clearly presented and easy to read.

1) Include an introduction to give a bit of background information — e.g. how you came to think of the project.

2) Use a mixture of media to present your project. It's always good to show off how good you are with CAD or that desktop publishing program, but don't forget about old-fashioned words to explain what you did, and sketches and prototypes to show how you did it.

3) Split up your evaluation into different sections to make it easy to read. Give each section a clear heading.

The sections could include:
a) how well your product satisfies the brief and specification
b) results from user trials
c) problems you encountered
d) improvements for the future

4) Think about how it fits together — your project needs to work *as a whole*. It should flow seamlessly from one bit to the next — don't just shove lots of separate bits in with no clue as to how they fit together.

Including photographs is great

Always take photos of any non-permanent work or intermediate stages in making the product. You can use either a normal or a digital camera and then either glue in the print or place the digital image into a word-processed document — whatever suits.

Photos are the only way of getting a lasting record of your work — and the examiners *REALLY WANT* you to do it.

You've done all the work — take time to show you've done it...

This is the time to really clock up those marks. And be experimental and creative when you're doing it. The aim is to make your project and your work easy to understand and attractive.

Tips on Presentation

Spelling and grammar might seem a bit insignificant once you've put all that work into your project. But they're really important and examiners notice them. You'll get marked down if you don't pay attention to detail in your presentation.

Vocabulary — use the right technical terms

BIG, IMPRESSIVE WORDS:

1) Do yourself a favour — learn all the technical terms.

2) And how to spell them.

3) And don't worry if you sound poncy.

4) Using the right technical terms impresses the examiners. They say so in their reports.

Also remember your grammar, spelling and punctuation

GRAMMAR, SPELLING, PUNCTUATION:

1) Treat your project like an English essay.

2) Get your spellings right. Double-check any words you often get wrong.

3) Remember to use full stops and capital letters and write in proper sentences.

4) Short sentences make your work clearer. Long sentences, with loads of commas, can often get very confusing, because it's easy, once you get to the end of the sentence, to forget what you were reading right at the start.

5) Structure your work in paragraphs — a new paragraph for a new topic.

ALWAYS read through your work after you've written it...

Of course your project has to look nice. Sloppy language and spelling can really put examiners off, before they've even started to think about the content. So get off on the right foot...

Summary Checklist

These things can really make your project a *winner*.
That's why it's got a whole extra page — so you can't forget any of it.
Before you hand in your project, make sure you've covered all of these bits,
and you'll be well on your way to D&T success.

Project Checklist

- [ ] 1) My design brief has lots of detail.
- [ ] 2) I've done plenty of research, and said why it's relevant.
- [ ] 3) I've made a detailed design specification.
- [ ] 4) I've come up with a wide range of project proposals.
- [ ] 5) I've included different ways of developing my product, and explained why I made my decisions.
- [ ] 6) I've tested my product on consumers.
- 7) I've done lots of planning, including:
  - [ ] a) a production plan (time plan),
  - [ ] b) planning for mass production.
- [ ] 8) I've evaluated my product throughout the project.
- [ ] 9) I've taken photos of intermediate stages and anything that won't last.
- [ ] 10) I've used a mixture of media to present my project.
- [ ] 11) I've checked my spelling and grammar.
- [ ] 12) I've used the right technical terms.

Practice Exam

Once you've been through all the questions in this book, you should feel pretty confident about the exam. As final preparation, here is a **practice exam** to really get you set for the real thing. This paper is designed to give you the best possible preparation for the differing question styles of the actual exams, whichever syllabus you're following. If you're doing Foundation then you won't have learnt every bit — but it's still good practice.

General Certificate of Secondary Education

GCSE
Design and Technology
Resistant Materials

Centre name					
Centre number					
Candidate number					

Time allowed: 2 hours

Surname
Other names
Candidate signature

In addition to this paper you will need:
- Drawing equipment
- Coloured pencils

Instructions to candidates
- Write your name and other details in the spaces provided above.
- Answer **all** questions in the spaces provided.
- Use blue or black ink or ball-point pen.

Information for candidates
- The marks available are given in brackets at the end of each question or part-question.
- The total number of marks available for this paper is **98**.
- There are **8** questions in this paper. There are no blank pages.
- Measurements are in millimetres unless stated otherwise.

Advice to candidates
- Work steadily through the paper.
- Include diagrams where they may be helpful.
- In calculations show clearly how you work out your answers.

Leave blank

1 This question is about the **scale of production**.

You should spend about 10 minutes on this question.

(a) Complete the table below by entering a description of each scale of production.
Name a typical product which is made by this method.
One example has been completed for you.

Scale of Production	Description	Product
One-off production	*A single product is made*	*The Eiffel Tower*
Batch production		
Mass production		
Continuous production		

(6 marks)

(b) Explain how the scale of production affects the cost of the product.

....

....

....

....

....

....

....

....

(6 marks)

AQA, 2005

Leave blank

2 This question is about **industrial practice.**

You should spend about 8 minutes on this question.

Fig. 1 shows a piece of round, mild steel bar. It has a machined spigot on one end.

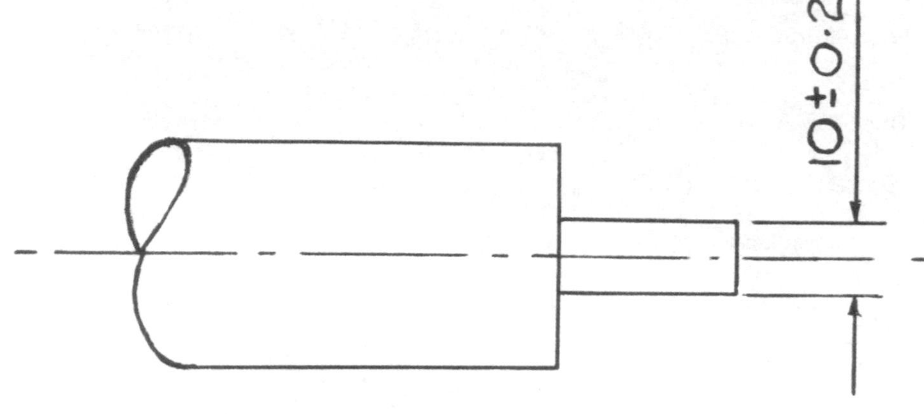

Fig. 1

(a) What is the **minimum** diameter of the spigot?

Minimum size: ....

(1 mark)

(b) What is the **maximum** diameter of the spigot?

Maximum size: ....

(1 mark)

(c) Name the tool that should be used to measure the spigot.

Tool: ....

(1 mark)

Leave blank

(d) Explain **one** advantage of using a gauge rather than the tool you have named in (c), when several of these components are to be made.

Advantage: ....

....
(2 marks)

(e) Explain the importance of 'tolerance' when manufacturing components.

....

....

....

....

....
(4 marks)

AQA, 2005

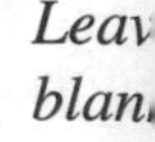

3 Fig. 2 shows an incomplete design for a tennis ball carrier to be made mainly from Medium Density Fibreboard (MDF). It is to be made in a school workshop.

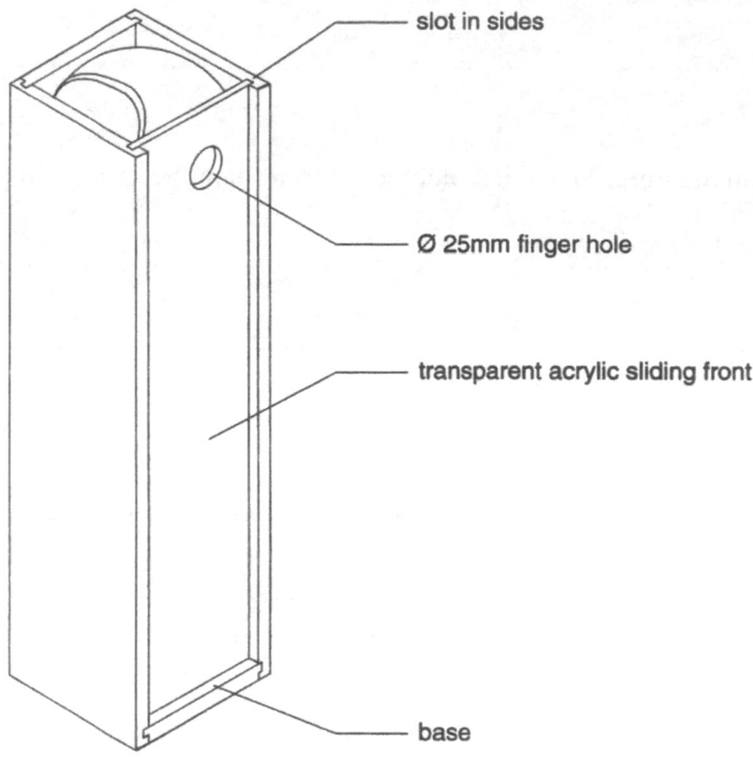

Fig. 2

(a) Complete the risk assessment table below identifying a **different** hazard and control measure for each process or activity. The first one has been completed for you.

Process/Activity	Hazard	Risk Assessment	Control measure
Sawing the MDF to size	Cut injury	Medium	• Both hands away from the cutting edge
Drilling the Ø 25 mm finger holes in the Acrylic		Medium	
Using a power router to make the slots in the MDF sides		High	

(4 marks)

Leave blank

(b) Use sketches and notes to design a handle for the tennis ball carrier.

The handle must:

- be ergonomically designed;
- allow easy access for the tennis balls;
- be fixed securely to the carrier.

Include details of:

- materials;
- construction;
- fittings;

used in your design.

(6 marks)

OCR, 2004

Leave blank

4 Fig. 3 shows a plastic notelet holder. The notelet holder is produced in quantity by injection moulding.

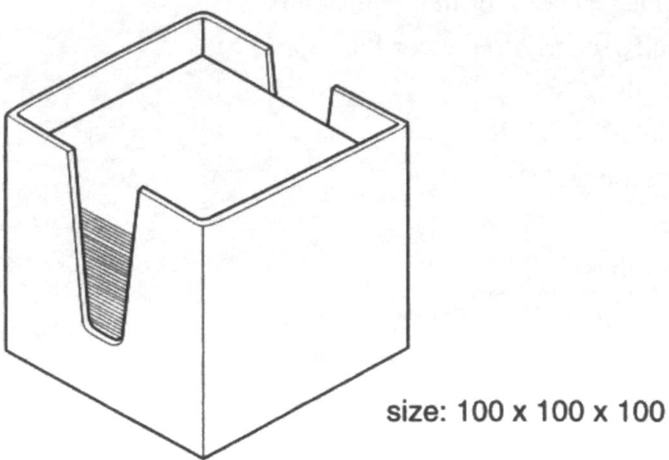

Fig. 3

(a) Explain why injection moulding is only cost-effective when products are manufactured in large quantities.

....

....

....

(2 marks)

(b) Quality control is an important part of manufacturing.
Describe **two** quality control checks that could be carried out during the manufacture of the injection moulded notelet holder.

1. ....

....

(1 mark)

2. ....

....

(1 mark)

Leave blank

(c) The notelet holder could also be made from a single piece of 3mm thick sheet plastic. Fig. 4 shows the development [net] for a notelet holder to be made from sheet plastic.

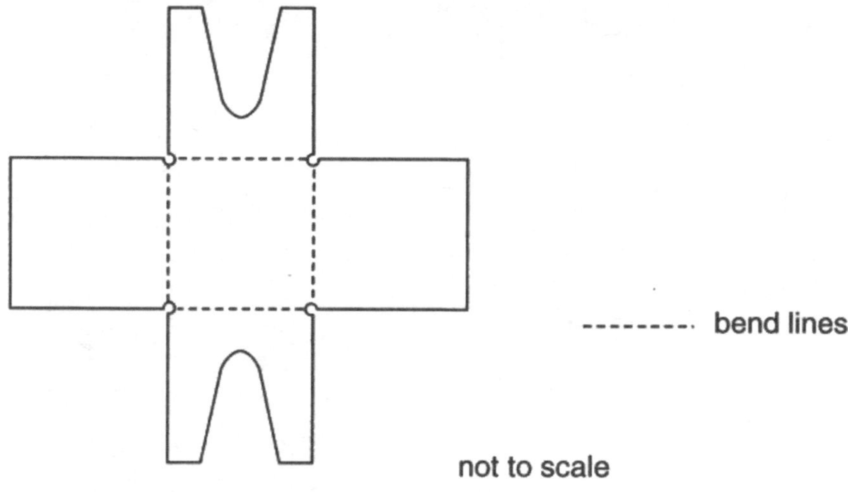

Fig. 4

(i) Describe how CAD/CAM could be used to help in the design and manufacture of this notelet holder.

....

....

....

(2 marks)

(ii) Name the software and computer-controlled machine you would use.

Software ....

(1 mark)

Computer-controlled machine ....

(1 mark)

(d) Both designs of notelet holder are to be manufactured in quantity.
Explain why injection moulding is a more environmentally-friendly process than making the notelet holder from sheet plastic.

....

....

....

....

(2 marks)

OCR, 2005

5 Fig. 5 shows a commercially produced toothbrush holder made from stainless steel.

Leave blank

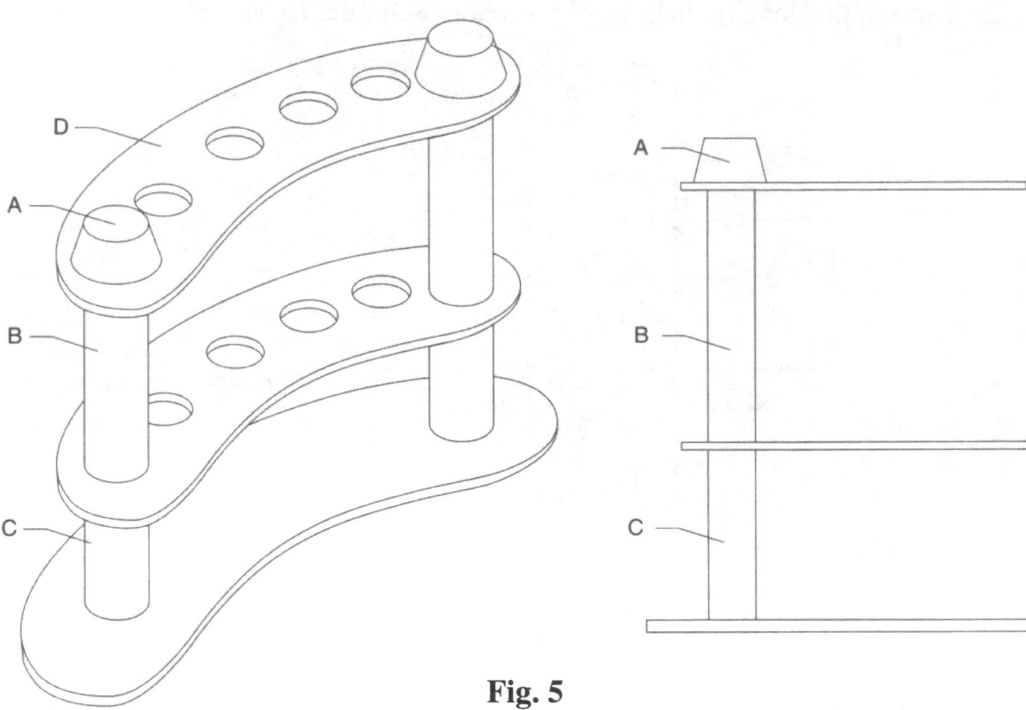

Fig. 5

(a) State **one** property of stainless steel that makes it difficult to work with.

....

(1 mark)

(b) Describe **two** functional design features of the toothbrush holder.

1. ....

....

(1 mark)

2. ....

....

(1 mark)

(c) State **two** reasons, other than the cost of stainless steel, why this toothbrush holder could be considered expensive to manufacture.

1. ....

....

(1 mark)

2. ....

....

(1 mark)

Leave blank

(d) Fig. 6 shows details of the toothbrush holder.
Each upright support is made from three separate pieces, **A**, **B** and **C**.

On the drawing below show how the three pieces could be connected to each other.
Add detailed notes to explain your method.

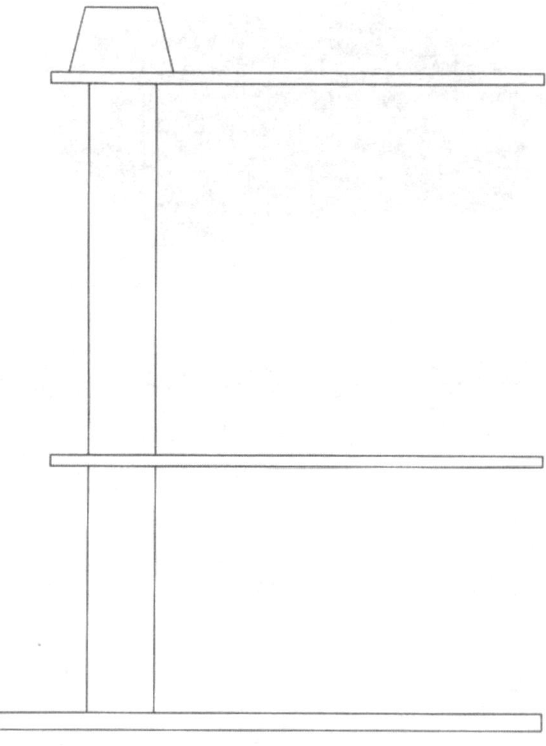

Fig. 6

(5 marks)

OCR, 2004

6 This question is about **industrial processes**.

Leave blank

You should spend about 10 minutes on this question.

Study Fig. 7 (a seed tray) below.

Fig. 7

(a) Name **one** suitable, **specific** material from which to make the seed tray.

Material: ....

(1 mark)

Fig. 8 shows a drawing of a former/mould used to vacuum form a similar seed tray to that as shown in Fig.7 above.

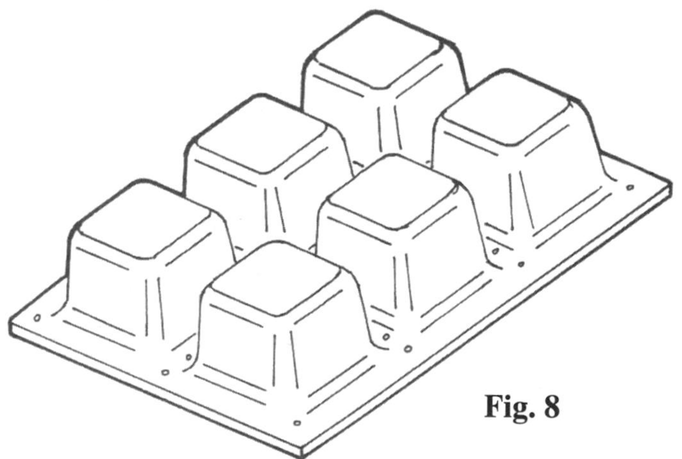

Fig. 8

Leave blank

(b) Use arrows and labels to indicate clearly **three** important features of the former/mould.
Explain the function of each feature.

Feature A: ....
(1 mark)

Explanation: ....

....
(2 marks)

Feature B: ....
(1 mark)

Explanation: ....

....
(2 marks)

Feature C: ....
(1 mark)

Explanation: ....

....
(2 marks)

(c) Name **one** suitable, **specific** material which could be used to make the former/mould.

Material: ....
(1 mark)

(d) Webbing/curtaining is a problem which can sometimes occur when vacuum forming.
Explain the likely causes of this problem.

Explanation: ....

....

....

....

....

....
(4 marks)

AQA, 2004

7 A company is designing a milk bottle holder to be left out on the doorstep to enable a delivery person to collect empty bottles and to deliver more milk.

Leave blank

The specification for the milk bottle holder is that it must:

- hold up to four bottles securely
- clearly indicate how many bottles are required to be delivered (1, 2, 3 or 4)
- be easy and safe to carry
- be easily suitable for production in batches of 50.

ADDITIONAL INFORMATION

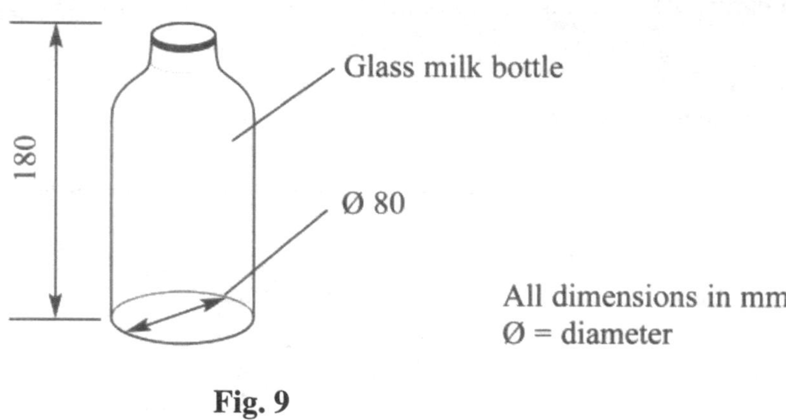

Fig. 9

(a) In the spaces below, use sketches and, where necessary, brief notes to show **two different** design ideas for the milk bottle holder which meet this specification. Do **not** evaluate your designs in part (a).

Design idea 1

(8 marks)

Leave blank

Design idea 2

(8 marks)

(b) Three of the original specification points are repeated below.
Evaluate how **one** of your design ideas succeeds or fails to meet each of the specification points.

Write the number of your chosen idea (1 or 2) here: ....

(i) The milk bottle holder must hold up to four bottles securely.

....

....

....

(2 marks)

(ii) The milk bottle holder must clearly indicate how many bottles are required to be delivered (1, 2, 3 or 4).

....

....

....

(2 marks)

(iii) The milk bottle holder must be easy and safe to carry.

....

....

....

(2 marks)

Edexcel, 2005

8 Fig. 10 shows details of a 'cross-head' water tap.
Some people find difficulty applying enough grip to turn the tap on or off.

Leave blank

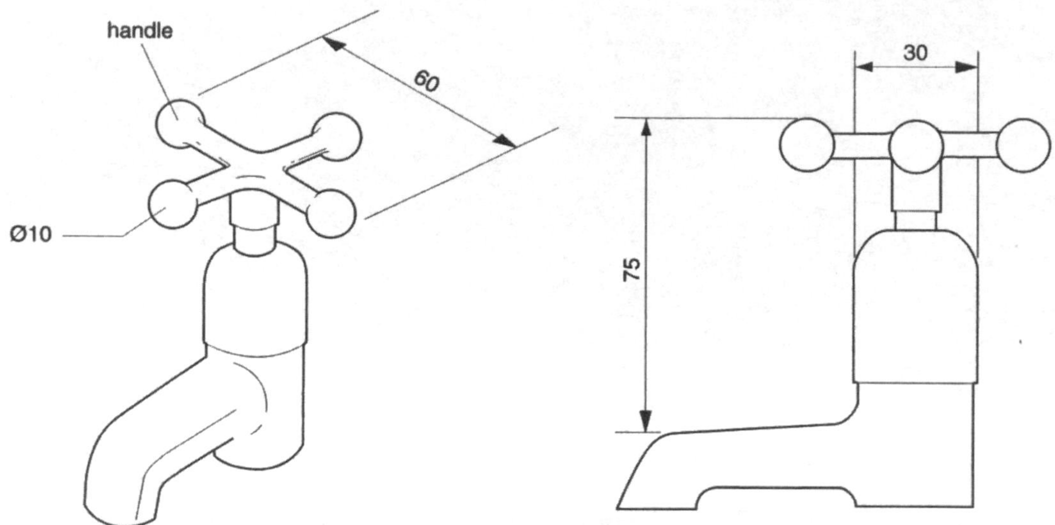

Fig. 10

(a) Use sketches and notes to develop a prototype design for a device that would make it easier for the tap to be turned on or off.
The prototype device must fit either over, under or across the handle of the 'cross-head' water tap.

(4 marks)

Leave blank

(b) Explain why ergonomic considerations are important to the success of your prototype device.

....

....

....
(2 marks)

(c) The prototype device would need to be trialled before the product is manufactured in quantity. Describe how trials of the prototype could be carried out.

....

....

....

....
(2 marks)

(d) The final design of the device is to be produced in quantity. Name the material from which your design could be made and the manufacturing process used.

Material ....
(1 mark)

Manufacturing process ....
(1 mark)

OCR, 2005

Leav
blan

END OF QUESTIONS

The answers to the warm-up questions haven't been included here — if there's any you don't know, the best way to learn them is to look back over the section. You can find all the answers there.

Page 10

2 (a) Possible answers: Where the cutlery storage tray will be put; the types of cutlery to be stored; the number and sizes of cutlery to be stored.
(2 marks — 1 for each piece of information.)

(b) Possible answers: Not enough compartments; tray is too shallow; compartments are the wrong size and shape.
(2 marks — 1 for each suggestion.)

(c) Two modifications should be suggested, to remedy the problems suggested in part (b). For example:
Make the tray deeper and add more compartments to hold different items.

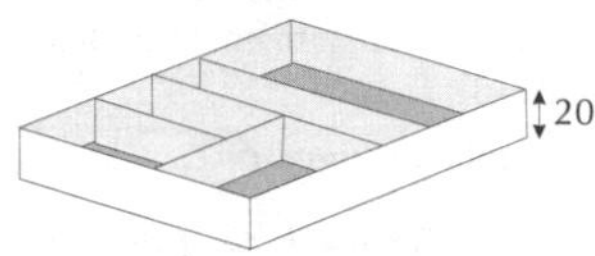

(4 marks — up to 2 marks for each modification.)

Make sure you add notes and labels to the sketch to explain the modifications — you won't get all the marks for just doing a sketch.

(d) Possible answers: Try pieces of cutlery in the tray; carry out a survey of people's views.
(2 marks — 1 for each suggestion.)

Page 11

3 Possible answers: must raise the computer user's feet; must not interfere with the use of the chair; must have a non-slip base; must have a non-slip top; must not damage the polished floor; must be strong enough to support the user's feet.
(4 marks — 1 for each condition.)

For questions like this, it's a case of racking your brain a bit and using common sense. Try to imagine it actually being used and think of potential problems if it was badly designed.

Page 19

2 Shaving thin layers of material; Bench plane
Cutting and shaping wood; (Wood) chisel
Shaping and smoothing material; File
Making holes; Brace
Making holes; Bradawl
Making large, flat-bottomed holes; Flat bit
(12 marks — 1 for each correct use or name.)

If you struggled with these, you need to go back and learn everything on page 13 and 14 again...

Page 25

2 Line bender or strip heater ***(1 mark)***

3 (a) Any thermoplastic other than acrylic, e.g. polythene ***(1 mark)***

(b)

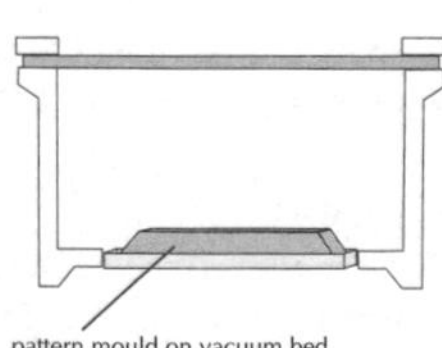

(3 marks — 1 mark for correct shape of mould, 1 for correct position, 1 for correct label.)

Page 34

2 From top to bottom: self-tapping screw; nail; woodscrew
(3 marks — 1 mark for each correct name.)

This question isn't as easy as looks. If you get any wrong, go back over pages 26 - 29. Make sure you understand exactly the meaning of terms like "tapered shank" and "clearance hole" — otherwise you'll never get it...

3

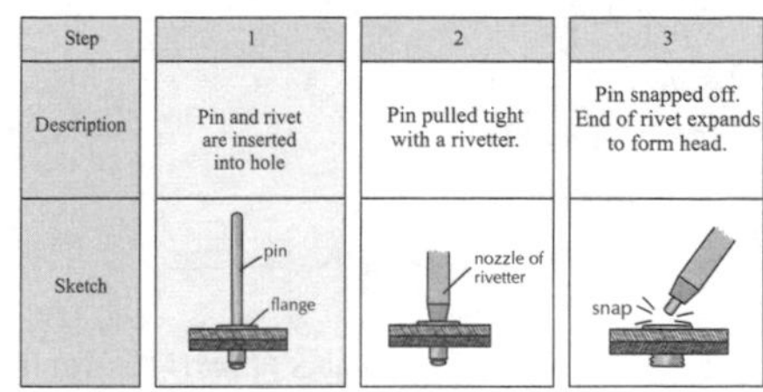

Step	1	2	3
Description	Pin and rivet are inserted into hole	Pin pulled tight with a rivetter.	Pin snapped off. End of rivet expands to form head.
Sketch	pin flange	nozzle of rivetter	snap

(5 marks — 2 for accurate sketches, 2 for accurate descriptions, 1 for correct sequence.)

Page 38

2 (a) It keeps the joint clean and prevents the surface from oxidising. ***(1 mark)***

(b) An unsuitable paint was used. ***(1 mark)***

(c) (i) E.g. cellulose paint ***(1 mark)***

(ii) It should be sprayed. ***(1 mark)***

Page 42

2 Possible points include:
Designs can be modelled and compared cheaply and easily;
Products can be viewed from all angles;
Products can be modelled in three dimensions;
Problems can be ironed out before production of prototypes;
Designs can be stored/distributed electronically;
Drawings are more accurate;
Common components can be duplicated, saving the need to redraw them each time;
Drawings can be edited without redrawing the whole thing.
(5 marks — 1 mark for each point made clearly.)

For a biggish question like this, it helps to quickly plan your answer. Jot ideas down the side until you've got five separate points, then write it out properly. Remember, you won't get 5 marks just by filling all the answer space — you've got to have 5 separate points.

3 The main points should be:
Produce a design for the door knobs on a computer (i.e. using CAD);
Set up a computer controlled lathe;
Download the control data from the computer to the lathe;
(3 marks — 1 mark for each point. Other suitable relevant points should also be accepted.)

Page 57

2 Many possible answers:
Hardness — files, drills, saws, router bits, spanners, knife blades.
Durability — outdoor items such as garden furniture, hinges, etc.
Compressive strength — bridge supports, chair and table legs, nails.
Toughness — armour, bulletproof vests, safety glasses, items to be bent into shape e.g. sheet steel.
Shear strength — rivets, screws, shelf ends.
(5 marks — 1 mark for each suitable example, with a maximum of 1 mark per property.)

3 (a) Various acceptable answers, for example:
polyethylene, PVC, polystyrene or other thermoplastic
(1 mark for naming 1 suitable material.)

(b) Various acceptable answers, for example:
melamine-formaldehyde, urea-formaldehyde or other thermosetting plastic
(1 mark for naming 1 suitable material.)

Page 58

4 (a) Possible answers include: aluminium is more lightweight than mild steel; aluminium does not rust, whereas mild steel will rust if not protected.
(2 marks — 1 mark for each suitable advantage.)

(b) Possible answers include: mild steel is cheaper than aluminium; mild steel is stronger than aluminium; mild steel can be fabricated and repaired using standard methods, whereas aluminium needs more specialised techniques.
(2 marks — 1 mark for each suitable advantage.)

(c) Possible answers include: carbon fibre — plastic reinforced with a woven matt of carbon fibres.
(2 marks — 1 mark for naming a suitable material, 1 mark for a good description.)

Page 64

2 (a) Exterior PVA glue *(1 mark)*

(b) (i) Epoxy resin (Araldite) *(1 mark)*

(ii) Interior PVA glue *(1 mark)*

(c) Acrylic cement (Tensol) *(1 mark)*

3 (a) Material Y *(1 mark)*

(b) In some ways, Z is a better choice as it is cheaper *(1 mark)* and unlike Y it is available in rods, a useful form from which to make the handle *(1 mark)*. However, Y could be said to be a better choice, as it is more attractive *(1 mark)* and has better corrosion resistance — important for use out of doors *(1 mark)*.

Page 72

2 (a) Once every 4 seconds (or 0.25 turns/second)

(2 marks — 2 marks for the correct final answer <u>OR</u> 1 mark for using the formula RPM of driven pulley = [RPM of driver pulley × diameter of driver pulley] ÷ diameter of driven pulley and putting the correct values in, i.e. [1 × 20] ÷ 80.)

(b) There are various correct answers. Driven sprocket should have half as many teeth as the driver sprocket. Here is one example.

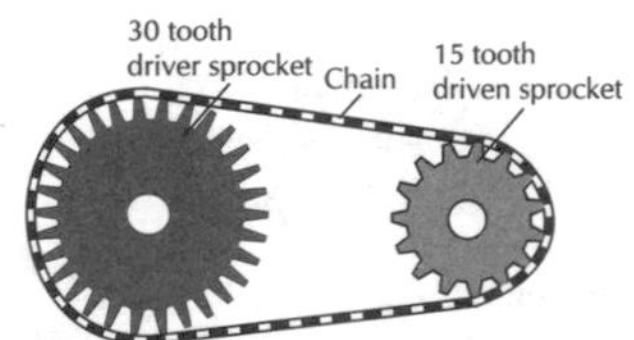

(4 marks — 2 marks for a correctly labelled drawing, 2 marks for getting the ratio of teeth correct.)

Page 78

2 (a) Answer should show a pear cam.

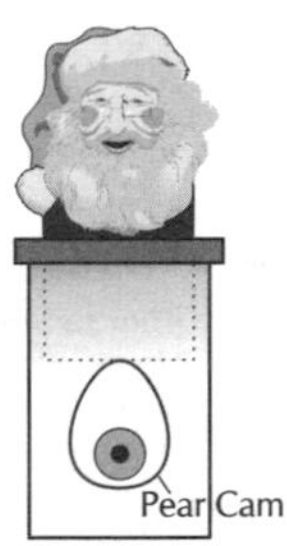

(2 marks — 1 mark for drawing a pear cam, 1 mark for drawing it in the correct position around the motor and the Father Christmas.)

(b) A pear cam *(1 mark)*

(c) Answer should show an offset circular cam, <u>OR</u> a crank.

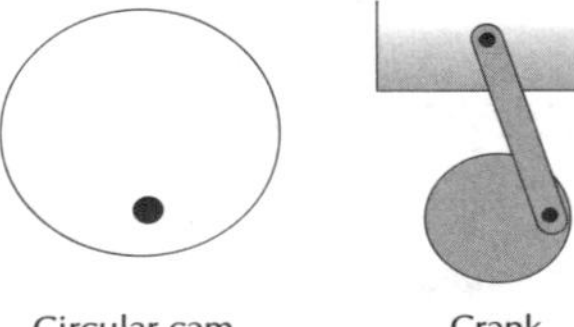

(1 mark)

(d) A circular cam / crank, as appropriate. *(1 mark)*

Page 85

2 There's more than one correct answer here. Here are two examples:

Notes: A micrometer is used to measure the diameter of each pipe. If the reading is between 29.8 mm and 30.2 mm, then the pipe is OK.

Notes: A double ended limit gauge could be used. One gauge measures 29.8 mm, the other 30.2 mm. Each pipe is tried in the gauges. If a pipe fits into the 30.2 mm gauge, but not the 29.8 mm gauge, then it's OK.

(3 marks — 1 mark for giving a method which would work, 1 mark for a clear sketch, 1 mark for a clear explanation.)

3 Possible answers include: to help get ideas for your new design; pick out good/bad examples of design/manufacture/material selection; learn how existing products work; get ideas on aesthetics; study relevant issues regarding ergonomics; compare costs of products.

(3 marks — one for each suitable suggestion.)

When designing a new product, you're always going to want to look at similar existing products to get ideas, and to work out which bits could be improved, etc. It makes perfect sense really...

Page 93

2 (a) The British Standards Institution *(1 mark)*

(b) The symbol shows that a product has met safety/quality/design standards. *(1 mark)*

3 (a) Ergonomic design means designing the size, proportions and function of a product so that it fits the needs of the user.

(2 marks — 1 mark for an incomplete answer.)

(b) Anthropometric data would have been used to work out the sizes of the main components of the chair, by allowing for human body measurements.

(2 marks — 1 mark for stating that the data would be used to work out important sizes, 1 mark for referring to human body measurements.)

(c) Many possible answers, for example:
designing the size of a desk to fit the user; designing the layout of a car so that the driver can reach all necessary controls.
(1 mark for a suitable example.)

"Ergonomic" and "Anthropometric" might be two very silly long words, but you'll definitely be asked about one (or both) of them in the exam. So make you sure you understand <u>exactly</u> what they mean.

Page 98

2 Many possible answers, for example:
apron, face mask, gloves, gauntlets, face visor, spats, body suits
(4 marks — 1 mark for each suitable item.)

3 Example answers: Risk assessment is a procedure carried out to identify and reduce the potential risks of using chemicals, machinery and equipment. OR Risk assessment is a procedure carried out on a product to identify and reduce any risks to the end user.
(2 marks — 1 mark only for an incomplete answer, e.g. "Risk assessment is the procedure of identifying risks".)

4 (a) If the wheels were detachable, there is a risk that the child would put one in their mouth *(1 mark)*, which would be a potential choking hazard. *(1 mark)*

(b) Many possible answers, for example:
The child may put the car in their mouth so the surface finish must be non-toxic; the car must not have sharp edges or the child may cut themself.
(2 marks — 1 mark for the safety aspect and 1 mark for explaining why it is necessary.)

Page 105

2 (a) (i) Cell production involves splitting production into individual components, each of which is made by a separate production cell. *(1 mark)* Each cell is a team of people, who are responsible for all aspects of production of their component. *(1 mark)*

(ii) Possible answers include: improved teamwork; good communication within the cell; improved quality
(1 mark for a suitable answer.)

(b) (i) Possible answers include:
jobbing production; batch production; flexible manufacturing
(2 marks — 1 mark for each suitable suggested production system.)

Jobbing production is fairly obvious here. Getting the other one is a bit trickier. If you ended up guessing, you need to go over pages 100-103 again. The answers are all in there...

(ii) Mass production involves breaking down the stages of production into simple repetitive tasks ***(1 mark)***. People are able to learn these tasks easily, and therefore don't need to be skilled ***(1 mark)***.

(c) Possible advantages include: no need to spend money on keeping large stockpiles of materials; not stockpiling materials means that you can save space; no risk of buying materials or components which won't get used.
(1 mark for one suitable advantage.)
Possible disadvantages include: requires time and effort spent on detailed forward planning; production must be kept on time or things will go wrong; production will be severely affected by any failures of suppliers to deliver materials on time.
(1 mark for one suitable disadvantage.)

Page 109

2 (a) Designer → Manufacturer → Retailer
(3 marks — 1 mark for each suitable role.)

(b) Client — identifies a need, gives the designer a brief, carries out market research and raises money for the project. OR Designer — develops client's ideas, sets out specification, produces detailed working drawings of final design. OR Manufacturer — plans and carries out manufacturing safely and efficiently to produce consistent results and make a profit. OR Retailer — gives customers what they want, at an affordable price. OR User — gets high quality product that works, fulfils a need and is good value for money.
(2 marks — 1 mark for an incomplete description, 2 marks for accurate description with level of detail shown above.)

Page 115

2 (a) A jig can speed up production ***(1 mark)*** and make it more accurate ***(1 mark)***.

(b) Many possible answers. Here is one example:

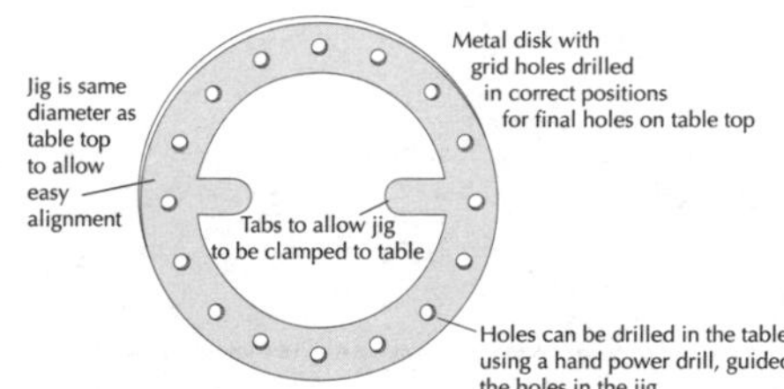

(6 marks — Up to 3 marks for clear and detailed drawing and up to 3 marks for good clear notes to explain use.)

This part is worth a whopping 6 marks, so don't rush it. Before you start, work out in your head (or in rough) exactly how it will look. Make sure your sketch is very clear with lots of labels explaining all the features.

Please note: The answers to the past exam questions have not been provided by or approved by the examining bodies (AQA, OCR and London Qualifications Ltd - Edexcel). As such, AQA, OCR and London Qualifications Ltd do not accept any responsibility for the accuracy or method of the working in the answers given. CGP has provided suggested solutions — other possible solutions may be equally correct.

Practice Exam Paper

1 a) Batch production — machinery can be used to make batches of different products — e.g. CD racks.
Mass production — Many identical products can be made — e.g. cars.
Continuous production — Non stop production 24/7 — e.g. oil.
(1 mark for each correct answer. Total of 6 marks for the question.)

b) One off production — mention: The unit cost is high because labour costs are high; a skilled workforce is needed; only a small number of products can be made; raw materials are expensive.
Batch production and mass production — mention: The unit cost is medium because CAM is used; a semi-skilled workforce is needed; work may be subcontracted.
Continuous production — mention: The unit cost is low because an unskilled workforce is needed; CAM is used extensively; intensive use of machinery 24 hours a day; intensive use of resources like buildings.
(1 mark for each correct answer. Total of 6 marks for the question.)

2 a) 9.8 ***(1 mark)***

b) 10.2 ***(1 mark)***

c) Possible answers: micrometer; vernier calliper. ***(1 mark for a correct tool.)***

d) Possible answers include: Less skill is needed by the user — this means semi-skilled or unskilled labour can be used to make the product;
It reduces the chance of a mistake, therefore there will be less wastage;
It is quicker than reading a micrometer, so it will take less time to make the product. ***(1 mark for stating an advantage, 1 mark for explaining the advantage. Total of 2 marks.)***

e) Possible answers include: It is very difficult to make a component exactly correct; It is easier to make a component within tolerances; It sets a maximum and minimum size that a component can be; A manufacturer knows its product will work if it is within tolerances. ***(2 marks for each point explained, up to 4 marks.)***

3 a) Any sensible hazard identified. Each hazard must be different. ***(1 mark for each hazard, up to 2 marks.)***
Any sensible control measure identified. Each control measure must be different. ***(1 mark for each control measure, up to 2 marks.)***

b) Any valid design acceptable. Award marks for:
Ergonomic considerations — shape, not too heavy etc. ***(1 mark)***;
Clear access — flexible, access from top etc. ***(1 mark)***;
Security of handle ***(1 mark)***;
Materials ***(1 mark)***;
Construction ***(1 mark)***;
Fittings ***(1 mark)***.

4 a) Possible answers include: injection moulding is only suitable for manufacturing in large quantities because of the high cost of the initial tooling ***(1 mark)***; large quantities need to be manufactured to recover the costs ***(1 mark)***. ***(1 mark for each valid point, up to 2 marks.)***

b) Possible answers include: random testing of material quality during manufacture; testing of product dimension tolerances; visual appearance to check quality of the production process. ***(1 mark for each valid point, up to 2 marks.)***

c) i) Possible answers include: CAD could be used to draw the shape of the net accurately or as a 3D image; CAM could be used to cut out the outline shape and engrave the bend lines. ***(1 mark for stating a use of CAD, 1 mark for stating a use of CAM. Up to 2 marks.)***

ii) Software — possible answers include: 2D Design; Pro-Desk Top. ***(1 mark)***
Computer controlled machine — possible answers include: CAMM 2; milling machine. ***(1 mark)***

d) If you make it from sheet plastic there is waste plastic after the net shape has been cut away. ***(1 mark)*** Injection moulding only uses the plastic granules needed for the notelet holder so there is minimal waste. ***(1 mark)***

5 a) It is very hard to work; surface finish is easily damaged.
(1 mark for a valid property)

b) Possible answers include: toothbrushes will not fall over; stability in use; easy to clean; materials will not rust; will accept different designs of toothbrush; individual space for each toothbrush.
(1 mark for each valid feature, up to 2 marks.)

c) Possible answers include: the shape is complex; it is made up of nine separate parts which adds to the cost; there would be a higher labour cost for the assembly of all the separate parts.
(1 mark for a sensible reason, up to 2 marks)

d) Possible method of connection: some form of pin or threaded rod for top and centre joints; some form of pin or threaded rod and rivets for the bottom joint.
(1 mark for giving a method of connection for each piece, award up to 2 marks for the quality of the technical detail, including whether the rods are separate pieces, how they fit etc. Total of 5 marks.)

6 a) Possible answers include: PVC; styrene; polycarbonate (PC); polypropylene (PP); HDPE; HIPS. *(1 mark)*

b) Possible answers:
Feature — rounded corners
Explanation — prevents thinning on the corners which avoids splitting the plastic. A rounded corner provides greater strength.
Feature — draft / tapered sides / sloping sides
Explanation — allows the former to be removed from the mould.
Feature — extraction holes
Explanation — allows the air to be removed from deep valleys which reduces the chance of webbing.
Feature — smooth sides
Explanation — helps the former to be removed from the mould. Provides a smooth finish to the mould.
(1 mark for each valid feature, up to 3 marks. 2 marks for each valid explanation, up to 6 marks. Total of 9 marks.)

c) Possible answers include: steel; aluminium; MDF; any suitable close grain hardwood. *(1 mark)*

d) Possible answers include: incorrect heating of the plastic; plastic may be too hot; plastic may be too cold; several formers have been placed too close together; extraction holes have not been used; the vacuum is not sealing correctly. *(1 mark for each valid point, up to 4 marks)*

7 a) Any valid design acceptable. Award marks for incorporating the following details:
Holding up to four bottles securely *(1 mark)*;
Evidence to indicate that bottles are held securely *(1 mark)*;
Evidence that the holder clearly indicates the number of bottles required *(1 mark)*;
Evidence that the numbers of bottles required can be changed *(1 mark)*;
Evidence to show it is easy to carry *(1 mark)*;
Evidence to show it is safe to carry bottles and they won't fall out *(1 mark)*;
Evidence that it's easily suitable for production in batches of 50 — use of tools/processes/machinery/specific material *(1 mark)*;
Use of jigs or templates *(1 mark)*.
To be awarded marks for Design 2 it must have different methods for each of the points above. *(Total of 16 marks)*

b) (i) Answer will give positive or negative aspects of the design in relation to its ability to hold up to 4 bottles *(1 mark)* and hold these bottles securely *(1 mark)*.

(ii) Answer will give positive or negative aspects of the design in relation to there being a clear indication of the number of bottles required *(1 mark)* and the ability for the number required to be changed *(1 mark)*.

(iii) Answer will give positive or negative aspects of the design in relation to it being easy to carry *(1 mark)* and it being safe to carry *(1 mark)*.

8 a) Any valid design acceptable.
Award marks for the following:
handle *(1 mark)*;
fitting to the tap *(1 mark)*;
ease of use *(1 mark)*;
additional detail *(1 mark)*;
(Total of 4 marks)

b) Without considering ergonomics people might not be able to use the device. It must relate to the human hand and the finger, wrist or arm operation of the tap.
(Or similar answer, 2 marks.)

c) Prototype trials involving getting individuals to try out the device and obtaining feedback about it, either through questionnaires or interviews.
(Or similar answer, 2 marks.)

d) Appropriate material named (e.g. various types of metal or plastic.)
(1 mark)
Appropriate process for the named material (e.g. aluminium — die cast; polypropylene — injection moulded.) *(1 mark)*

Working out your Grade

- *Find your average percentage for the whole exam.*
- *Look it up in this table to see what grade you got. If you're borderline, don't push yourself up a grade — the real examiners won't.*

Average %	85+	74 – 84	61 – 73	47 – 60	37 – 46	29 – 36	22 – 28	15 – 21	under 15
Grade	A*	A	B	C	D	E	F	G	U

Important
- *This is a Higher paper — if you're doing Foundation, you'll need more marks in the real exam. E.g. you'll generally need 26 marks or more to get a G grade.*
- *Obviously these grades are only a guide, and the more practice you do the better...*

Index

Index

Index

Let's face it, you want CGP Revision Books — not other people's dreary stuff.

Everyone else just gives you dreary revision books with only the boring stuff in and no entertainment. Boo. Hiss. We're different — we always try and make sure you're gonna enjoy using our books.

What you ***really*** need is a ***Free Catalogue*** showing the full range of CGP Revision Books. That way you can be sure you're not missing out on a brilliant book that ***might just save your life***.

At CGP we ***work our socks off*** to despatch your stuff really quickly.
If you get your order to us before 5.00pm (Mon-Fri) you should get it next day — most of the time, anyway.
(Obviously, if you order on Saturday night on a bank holiday weekend then you won't get it 'til Wednesday morning at the very earliest — no matter how hard we try!)

FIVE ways to get your Free Catalogue really quickly

- Phone: 0870 750 1252 (Mon-Fri, 8.30am to 5.30pm)
- Fax: 0870 750 1292
- E-mail: orders@cgpbooks.co.uk
- Post: CGP, Kirkby in Furness, Cumbria, LA17 7WZ
- Website: www.cgpbooks.co.uk

CGP books — available in all the best bookshops

TRS41